PRAISE FOR *THE PANORAMIC LEADER*

"*The Panoramic Leader* offers a timely, practical road map for leaders who face unprecedented complexity and must still bring out the best in others. With vivid stories and grounded wisdom, Choe and Goldsmith show how expanding your field of vision and listening deeply to stakeholders can transform your decision-making, along with the culture and performance of your organization."

Amy C. Edmondson, Novartis Professor of Leadership at Harvard Business School and author of *Right Kind of Wrong: The Science of Failing Well*

"*The Panoramic Leader* is one of those rare books that makes you pause and reflect. It's a powerful, practical companion to becoming not just a more effective leader but also a better human being. For leaders seeking to make better decisions when it matters most, listen more deeply, and lead others with wisdom and heart, this book is an essential guide."

Chester Elton, *New York Times* bestselling coauthor of *The Carrot Principle* and *Leading with Gratitude*

"In a world that valorizes specialization, *The Panoramic Leader* makes the case for developing multidimensional vision. This book will help leaders see more—and, equally important, see differently."

Daniel H. Pink, #1 *New York Times* bestselling author of *The Power of Regret* and *Drive*

"In a world obsessed with short-term results, *The Panoramic Leader* invites us to step back and see the bigger picture. Cornelia Choe and Marshall Goldsmith offer a framework for leading with clarity, courage, and long-term purpose—a refreshing reminder that true leadership begins with perspective."

Dorie Clark, *Wall Street Journal* and *USA Today* bestselling author of *The Long Game*

"*The Panoramic Leader* challenges long-held assumptions about leadership, especially the idea that we're meant to have all the answers, all the time. Cornelia Choe and Marshall Goldsmith invite us to embrace a new kind of leadership grounded in listening and the courage to keep evolving alongside uncertainty. They capture a powerful truth: leaders grow stronger when they open themselves to others' perspectives and pivot in response to new understanding. This is a timely guide, calling on us all to think and lead in entirely new ways."

Francine Katsoudas, Chief People, Policy, and Purpose Officer and Executive Vice President of Cisco

"Remarkable leaders don't just act differently; they see differently. This book shows how perspective becomes power in a world of constant change."

Guy Kawasaki, Chief Evangelist of Canva, former Chief Evangelist of Apple, and *New York Times* bestselling author of *Enchantment*

"Cornelia Choe and Marshall Goldsmith have given us a remarkable framework for leadership development that blends wisdom with practicality, helping leaders see with greater clarity, connect with deeper humanity, and act with grounded wisdom. *The Panoramic Leader* is about how we choose to engage with the world around us and how we can do so with empathy and purpose."

Hubert Joly, former CEO of Best Buy and bestselling author of *The Heart of Business*

"This book will punch you in the gut, in the best way. *The Panoramic Leader* is a wake-up call to stop leading in silos and start making decisions with the full picture. Cornelia and Marshall show how real power comes not from control, but from connection. Read this if you're serious about co-elevation, not just managing optics."

Keith Ferrazzi, *New York Times* bestselling author and globally recognized authority on leadership, team performance, and the future of work

"*The Panoramic Leader* offers a compelling vision for leadership grounded in integrity, clarity, and purpose. Cornelia Choe and Marshall Goldsmith remind us that effective leadership is not simply about intelligence or experience but about seeing the world and the people in it with empathy and wisdom. This book is both timely and timeless."

Kenneth C. Frazier, former Chairman and CEO of Merck & Co., Inc., and Chairman of Health Assurance Initiatives at General Catalyst

"*The Panoramic Leader* challenges us to see beyond the narrow confines of short-term results and individual ambition. Choe and Goldsmith remind us that leadership, at its best, is about widening our lens—to include people and purpose in every decision."

Paul Polman, former CEO of Unilever and coauthor of *Net Positive*

"In an AI world, where content is commoditized, the ability to see broadly, connect context, and shape direction is becoming the defining capability of leadership. This is not just an individual leadership skill but an organizational capability that leaders everywhere can no longer afford to overlook. *The Panoramic Leader* shows not only why this is critical but also how one can build this muscle in a thoughtful way."

Piyush Gupta, former Group CEO of DBS Bank, Chairman of Temasek India and Mandai Park Holdings, and Chairman of the Board of Trustees of Singapore Management University

"Panoramic vision—the ability to see around the corners—is an essential skill in a world turned upside down. Leaders will need to cultivate it and to seed its growth throughout their organizations. Fortunately, *The Panoramic Leader* offers a clear map for fostering broad-spectrum capacity, in ourselves and in those we lead."

Sally Helgesen, bestselling author of *How Women Rise* and *Rising Together*

"Cornelia Choe and Marshall Goldsmith offer a framework that's both intellectually rigorous and deeply human. *The Panoramic Leader* shows how expanding awareness—of self, others, and systems—transforms not only our leadership but our impact."

Tasha Eurich, organizational psychologist and *New York Times* bestselling author of *Bankable Leadership*

"With vivid stories and the innovative GEM framework, this book will help you see the world—and yourself—in a whole new light. Choe and Goldsmith reveal a fresh, deeply human approach to thinking, deciding, and leading in a time when perspective is every leader's greatest advantage."

Todd Cherches, CEO of BigBlueGumball and author of *VisuaLeadership: Leveraging the Power of Visual Thinking in Leadership and in Life*

THE PANORAMIC LEADER

HOW GREAT LEADERS SEE **DIFFERENTLY**

CORNELIA CHOE
MARSHALL GOLDSMITH

100 COACHES
PUBLISHING
AN IMPRINT OF AMPLIFY PUBLISHING GROUP

100 COACHES
PUBLISHING
AN IMPRINT OF AMPLIFY PUBLISHING GROUP

www.amplifypublishinggroup.com

The Panoramic Leader: How Great Leaders See Differently

For more information, please contact:
Amplify Publishing, an imprint of Amplify Publishing Group
620 Herndon Parkway, Suite 100
Herndon, VA 20170
info@amplifypublishing.com

Library of Congress Control Number: 2025927714

CPSIA Code: PRFRE0526A

ISBN-13: 979-8-89138-834-5

Printed in Canada

To our families, whose love and laughter remind us what leadership is truly for.
And to Alan Mulally and panoramic leaders everywhere, who expand our field of vision and elevate us all.

CONTENTS

Foreword

A few years ago, I had just finished a conversation with a young CEO who was growing her company at breathtaking speed. She was hiring, building, launching—doing everything right.

What struck me most wasn't her strategy but her self-awareness.

She said, "Every week I learn something that changes how I see the whole picture. My job is to keep learning faster than the world is changing around me."

That line stayed with me. That's leadership today: learning faster than the world changes, without losing your humanity. In our book *Blitzscaling*, Chris Yeh and I dubbed these kinds of people "infinite learners," after their ability to unlearn the lessons of past success in order to better learn the lessons that lead to future success.

That insight came to mind again when I read Cornelia and Marshall's *The Panoramic Leader*. They're sharp thinkers and thoughtful builders—people who not only study leadership but help so many practice it at the highest levels. What they've built in these pages is both practical and deeply human.

I especially appreciate their belief, which I strongly share, that leadership is a team sport, not an individual one. Far too many books focus on what a leader should do as an individual, rather than explaining how a leader can build a powerful network around themselves.

The GEM model that Cornelia and Marshall lay out in this book—*Get Up Close, Establish Meaningful Bonds, Map Your Evolving Perspective*—is deceptively simple. Yet it encodes a truth I've seen again and again in the best leaders, whether at start-ups, global companies, or nonprofits: they listen deeply, build trust across boundaries, and never stop refining their understanding. They leverage what my book *The Alliance* calls "Network Intelligence" to gain a panoramic perspective based on the wisdom of people they know and trust.

When I think back to the early days of LinkedIn or about the leaders and entrepreneurs I work with now like Satya Nadella of Microsoft, Dr. Siddhartha Mukherjee of Manas AI, and Alice Bentinck of Entrepreneur First, some of the most important successes come from the moments when someone's perspective widened because of this network intelligence—when a founder saw their team as co-creators or an engineer reframed a problem from a customer's point of view. Those are panoramic moments, and they change everything downstream from them.

Cornelia and Marshall have taken that intuition and turned it into a powerful framework. They show us that curiosity, empathy, and reflection—often dismissed as "soft skills"—are actually the hard infrastructure of modern leadership. This scaffolding allows trust to compound and insight to spread.

I also love how this book extends beyond the professional sphere. *Panoramic thinking* isn't just a leadership technique—it's a life practice. It sharpens your capacity to see patterns, to connect people and ideas, to bring more of the world into focus. It applies as much to a family dinner or a friendship as it does to a boardroom or an all-hands meeting.

The world will keep accelerating. Complexity will only increase. But the leaders who thrive will be the ones who keep expanding their field of vision, who can see the system and the soul at the same time.

Cornelia and Marshall have given us a guide for leading with awareness, connection, and courage.

If leadership is the art of seeing further—and helping others see with you—then *The Panoramic Leader* is the telescope we need right now.

—Reid Hoffman,
cofounder of LinkedIn,
Inflection AI, and Manas AI

PART ONE

THE FOUNDATIONAL SHIFT: UNDERSTANDING YOUR MAP AND MINDSET

CHAPTER 1

The Missing Piece

"I've been put in an extremely difficult position. I feel like my world's been turned upside down, and the ground just keeps shifting," Mike candidly shared with his peers. "Some of my employees are panicking. They want to know what's coming next—I can't tell them yet."

Mike had joined one of Cornelia's Leaders' Circles—a select group of senior business leaders with distinct strategic experience who came together to exchange ideas and learn from one another. Every member of the circle was wrestling with a tremendously difficult issue.

Cornelia had known Mike for some time, and he had a naturally easygoing disposition—quick with a laugh and usually brimming with confidence. But on this particular day, the stress and confusion he was feeling were unmistakable, the bright sunlight streaming into the room accentuating the fatigue written deeply on his face.

As general manager of the US market—the largest and most critical for the company—Mike found himself confronted with a bold but necessary decision from headquarters to fundamentally transform their product line. Until then, the company had thrived on a series of successful niche offerings and had long been the market leader. But smaller, more nimble competitors started using AI to offer real-time customization, and they were slicing into the company's market share. Now, sales were dropping so fast that the company's survival was at risk.

In response, the business's top brass made the decision to dramatically change their portfolio of products and sell related services. That was going to require Mike to implement some major changes, including a restructuring that would force him to lay off several of his executive team members, as well as much of the staff, and bring in new talent.

"I've taken a hard look at each member of my team to determine if they're still a fit," he said, lowering his voice, which accentuated the creaking of his chair as he leaned forward. "You know, it's not like I haven't done this before. I've done restructurings. But the scale this time is making the process personally devastating to me."

Mike had been bottling up a great amount of emotion and was relieved to finally open up about it.

He felt so strongly about his team because they'd worked together for more than a decade. In fact, he'd worked with many of them since his early days with the organization as a new manager. They'd shown him the ropes and remained loyal to him when he was promoted above them. He had great respect for that loyalty because it was a value that he treasured. "I've always prided myself on being extremely loyal," Mike explained. "It's one of the qualities that brought me to the position I'm in. It's a large part of my success. What's more, my team deserves it from me."

Making the situation even harder for Mike was that only the first phase of the transformation, which involved budget cuts, had been announced, and he wasn't free to inform his team of the layoffs that were next on the agenda. He knew people were anticipating a restructuring. They felt a great deal of anxiety about their job security and were confused about whether they should start looking for new work. With team members pressing Mike for information, the secrecy imposed by headquarters was weighing heavily on him. He believed in transparency, and he hated that his actions were making them struggle with so much uncertainty.

Mike was also deeply troubled because the company's new strategy had simply been handed down to him from on high. He hadn't been consulted, and he disagreed with elements of the plan that overlooked the unique dynamics of his team. He knew other general managers also had objections, and he resented the lack of opportunity to share this input with headquarters. His own leadership style was more democratic, and he strongly believed that this recent top-down approach was misguided.

To make matters even more frustrating, headquarters was being "shifty" with him. At first, he was instructed to cut 20 percent of his budget, and then the number was abruptly increased to 30 percent, with no explanation. And earlier, he'd been told to begin the first phase of the transformation in three months, only to have the deadline cut to two months—again, with no explanation. Clearly the team at headquarters was grappling with logistics regarding the strategy, but Mike was being kept in the dark. That made him feel they didn't trust him and also that his own job might be at risk.

With the rapidly changing mandates and lack of information, Mike felt overwhelmed with all the unknowns—not only for his teams but for his own future with the company—and he was finding it very difficult to plan the path forward. With no guarantee that he wouldn't also be booted as part of the restructuring, he wondered if making the leap to another company might be the smartest thing to do.

Mike sighed. Yes, all of his recent irritations with headquarters were very distracting, but his sense of loyalty to the firm made him feel that jumping ship would be a betrayal of the trust of his team and the faith of the higher-ups who had consistently supported and promoted him throughout his tenure. They needed him to pull off this transition.

"I need to decide the best way to resolve this," Mike said, looking out at the other executives in his circle. He was feeling stymied, almost frozen by his conflicting beliefs and roiling emotions. At the heart of Mike's dilemma was the mental map he'd developed that guided his leadership.

The Maps That Guide Us

We all have a map in our minds that we've drawn and use as part of our internal GPS to help us make decisions in our lives. This map includes an overview of the landscape of challenges and opportunities around us. It also includes lessons we've learned throughout our lives starting from early childhood, the values our families taught us, the norms of the culture we grew up in, discoveries we made, and our battle scars from hard knocks endured along the way.

Our map also includes all our experiences from our work lives—takeaways from how we've been managed and from managing others, lessons we've learned from successes and failures, and pitfalls we've learned to avoid.

Whenever we face a new challenge—or find a new opportunity—we turn to our mental map, looking for experiences that might show us how best to move forward.

However, the relentless pace of technological advances, shifting geopolitics, public health crises, environmental challenges, and economic transitions reshapes our world so quickly that it can feel overwhelming, leaving parts of our maps incomplete or outdated. This was true for Mike's map, making it impossible for him to see a clear path forward. He needed new perspectives from people who could see his predicament in different ways and help him update his map.

When faced with difficult decisions, we can easily fall into the trap of believing we should have all the answers—or at least appear as if we have them. This is especially true if we're in a leadership role. The thing is, none of us has all the answers. To consistently make the very best decisions, we must look outward as well as inward. We need to consider a wider range of experiences and opinions—coming to us from a full 360 degrees—to panoramically see our way through difficult challenges.

In other words, we must fill in the missing pieces of our maps.

From the outside looking in, you might think that most executives are successful because they naturally make great decisions. Sure, some executives do seem to have a magic wand, where everything they touch turns to gold. We—Cornelia and Marshall—have had the distinct privilege and pleasure of working with many of these highly successful people over the past several decades. However, the real story is that far more executives than you might expect fail to see a clear path forward.

According to research published by the Corporate Executive Board, at least half—somewhere between 50 percent and 70 percent—of new executives fail within their first eighteen months on the job.[1] That number is as shocking as it is catastrophic, for both the leaders who are affected by this silent epidemic and for the organizations they lead.

Which brings us to the crucial question: Why are these executives failing?

We've spent most of our lives working with senior leaders globally in business, government, and nonprofit organizations, and from what we've seen, the biggest problem for leaders today is that they're having a harder time making effective decisions than ever before.

It's not that they aren't talented decision makers. They usually are. But with the scope and speed of change in the world today, leaders are struggling mightily to understand—or even see—the whole panorama of stakeholders, events, innovations, and ideas affecting them. When they cling too tightly to their own fixed perspectives, they risk heading down the wrong paths and making decisions that pull them further from their goals.

If we were to write a book on what leaders do (and Marshall has written more than one or two on that topic), decision-making would be one of their key duties. Whether it's bet-the-company decisions, such as merging with a rival firm, or more typical challenges like launching a new product, leaders are constantly called on to make tough decisions and tradeoffs.

The problem is that so many of the decisions leaders make aren't good ones. McKinsey & Company looked at the decisions made by senior executives and came up with some sobering news. According to their survey, 72 percent of senior executives reported that bad strategic decisions were being made as often as good ones or were the norm.[2]

Leaders don't fail for lack of intelligence. They fail because they're navigating with partial maps. We call this perspective blindness—the tendency to mistake an incomplete view of reality for the whole. In an increasingly volatile world, that mistake compounds quickly. Panoramic leadership is a strategic advantage.

Three Big Challenges for Leaders Today

In our own experience working with senior leaders, we've found three big challenges in today's global business environment that get in the way of their ability to make good decisions.

Challenge 1: Overwhelming Change

Leaders today are pressured by the increasing rate and intensity of change. In the span of just a few years, we've faced a relentless wave of disruptions including economic swings, technological advances, and global crises. The weight of all this change is becoming unbearable. It's not just our minds playing tricks on us.

The only thing keeping many of us afloat is the thought—the hope—that we're going to get a break from all these challenges, that a calmer future is just over the horizon. But the weather forecast, in the form of Korn Ferry's CEO & Board Survey 2025, warns that the storm is far from over. It is, in fact, getting worse. When leaders were asked about risk, "a startling 63 percent said their organization's risk exposure had jumped in the past 12 months," with pressure coming from all sides, in the form of AI, geopolitical conflicts, and talent and skills gaps.[3]

Change isn't just moving faster—it's also overlapping and, at times, even conflicting. Before we've had the chance to fully address one challenge, another begins, followed quickly by more. Each new change ripples out and collides with others. It's like dominoes falling in all different directions.

Challenge 2: An Increasingly Integrated World

A single event in one region or country can affect hundreds of millions, even billions, of people in countries around the globe. Our interconnectedness causes individuals and organizations to be impacted by significant, unpredictable ripple effects that make an accurate understanding of the landscape elusive and good decision-making much more challenging.

We got a wake-up call about this with the 2008 financial crisis. The downturn in the US housing market triggered defaults on mortgages, spreading contagion through a global chain reaction of failing international investments in mortgage-backed securities and other assets. The result was the catastrophic knock-on effects of the collapse of international financial institutions, contracted global trade, and recession in many countries around the world.[4] According to a 2009 statement by Ben Bernanke, an American economist and chairman of the US Federal Reserve at the time, "Financial disruptions do not respect borders. The crisis has been global, with no major country having been immune."[5]

As the world becomes ever more interconnected, having the ability to anticipate, adapt to, and manage these ripple effects is no longer optional.

Challenge 3: An Increasing Range of Stakeholders

Leaders are now expected to address the interests of a wider range of stakeholders. From the 1970s until recently, leaders primarily focused on shareholders, due to the doctrine of shareholder primacy.[6] Delivering short-term profits and investor returns drove decision-making. The dangers of that "short-termism" have become apparent, however: Companies often overlooked opportunities with longer-term payoffs.

As former CEO of Unilever Paul Polman and writer Andrew Winston explained in the *Harvard Business Review*, "Serving only shareholders overlooks a fundamental reality: You have to please customers, attract and retain talent, and work with communities and suppliers to create valuable enterprises. Long-term resilience and business survival depend on sustainably serving stakeholders and society."[7]

Yet stakeholders have competing interests—a dynamic that creates even more complexity for leaders. In 2014, after facing pressure from Greenpeace over Shell's Arctic drilling, Lego decided not to renew its long-standing partnership with the energy company. Caught between the conflicting interests of two different stakeholders, the company announced, "The Lego brand . . . should never have become part of Greenpeace's dispute with Shell."[8]

What's more, the composition of stakeholder groups has become more varied. An executive working in France might report to company headquarters in the Netherlands while also needing to coordinate with Singaporean colleagues in the morning and then team members in California in the evening. Just scheduling meetings is a challenge! But each of these groups of employees may also have different views about the right way to develop a new product or the best model for sales. This, of course, means exponentially greater complexity for business leaders and the teams who work with them.

The solution to all three of these challenges? To get better information—the *right* information—needed to make good decisions.

Tuning In to What Matters Most

Ironically, we have more data available to us than ever before. But much of it is conflicting, misleading, or simply distracting. As a result, we can't see clearly through the fog. This can lead us to focus only on the part of the landscape we do see clearly—acting only on that information—at the expense of making needed changes that reside in those "foggy" areas of our perception.

For example, the communications app Skype was once so popular it was a verb, but by 2015, competition from WhatsApp and Snapchat had eroded its dominance, especially among younger users. Microsoft, which owned the service, revamped the platform. In doing so, the company excessively focused on the look of the app and on creating features, neglecting to improve its service reliability.

A flashy 2017 redesign was intended to make the service look cooler.

A number of the popular features of the competitors were added, such as "mojis"—short TV and movie clips—and a Snapchat-style feature called "highlights," which made "disappearing" photos and videos available to share with selected contacts. But those new features were unpopular—users found them difficult to navigate—and the redesign missed Skype's core objective of providing users with a dependable communication platform. Then, when COVID-19 hit, making reliable video communication essential, millions of users jumped ship to Zoom and WhatsApp, a shift that ultimately led to Skype's retirement in 2025.[9]

Many leaders are surprised to discover that another potential roadblock in our quest to obtain the right data is gatekeepers—the well-intentioned people who guard precious access to our time: executive assistants, chiefs of staff, and other advisers. They screen messages, sort through a daily myriad of requests, and help establish priorities. Yet whether to manage agendas, reduce overload, or promote what they believe is most relevant, these gatekeepers may filter out important people and information. The result is that leaders often miss opportunities to gather valuable insights.

Others try to actively "filter" what we see, either to please us, because they want to make themselves look good, or to avoid delivering bad news. This filtering means that we often miss important insights from those around us.

We're often given the advice to get on the balcony so we can survey the dance floor, meaning we should step back to get a big-picture perspective.[10] This is extremely helpful advice and should be our first step.

In times of constant and unpredictable change, however, when we get to the balcony, there may be so many people on the dance floor that we can't see through the swirl of activity to spot important events. We may perceive that everything's going well even as some troublemakers quietly infiltrate the party.

To get a meaningful panoramic view and spot significant developments, it's important to invite others up to the balcony with us. We've got to consult with people who understand varied aspects of the complex dynamics we're contending with—people who see the world differently—and can add their perspectives to our maps. They may already know the majority of the guests and help us notice that the party's being taken over by gatecrashers.

To help leaders get on the balcony with others who understand different dynamics on the dance floor, Cornelia brings together small groups of carefully selected leaders—whom she calls *peers*—in her Leaders' Circles. Together, they work through issues that are critical to their companies' success, and sometimes to their own survival as top executives, just like the restructuring challenge Mike faced. Connecting with peers who have shouldered comparable responsibilities, have grappled with similar challenges, and yet bring different experiences and perspectives is essential to gaining deeper insights into our problems and seeing the full panorama of possibilities.

These leaders often uncover the real issues that lie beneath their initial diagnosis by sharing their challenges openly with trusted peers. In one Leaders' Circle, a newly appointed CEO, formerly the COO, was struggling to understand why employee engagement remained particularly low in certain areas of the company, especially the marketing department. Having built his career in operations, he was unfamiliar with the dynamics of some other departments and, as a result, was misreading their cues.

The peers in his Leaders' Circle weren't convinced by his framing of the problem, and they shared many other potential reasons for disengagement beyond the "unmotivated" employees that he saw. They recommended that he conduct an in-depth listening tour with department heads to hear, without judgment or agenda, the real challenges they faced. These meetings exposed a web of deeper issues—including delayed decisions and blurred accountability—prompting the leader to initiate transformative, company-wide change, starting with rebuilding trust and cohesion within his senior leadership team.

Sometimes to get the information we need, we must leave the balcony and step onto the dance floor. By working the floor and talking to lots of guests, including the uninvited ones, we can make vital discoveries that give us a clearer understanding of what's really happening and what to do next.

If we want to grow our panoramic leadership, we need to get up close and speak with lots of different stakeholders, both inside and outside the organization, and incorporate their viewpoints into our maps. This may be uncomfortable at first, because the information we discover doesn't always confirm what we want to believe. But surprising news is often the most valuable news.

At a Leaders' Circle meeting, Kate, an executive recently promoted into a demanding role, shared her frustrations about the lack of support she was getting from a few colleagues. When one of her peers asked whether this was an attempt to sideline her influence, she contemplated this unsettling possibility—but after weighing the situation, responded that although difficult, things hadn't gone that far. But the question lingered in her mind.

When she returned to work, she reached out to some of her key stakeholders and discovered that quiet efforts were underway to undermine her reputation. Kate brought this conflict out into the open, and within weeks, the dynamics shifted. At the next circle meeting, she expressed her gratitude to the group for their candor in challenging her perspective and motivating her to act before the situation escalated.

Experiences like these remind us that true panoramic leadership isn't just about seeing more—it's about seeing *differently*: noticing what's been overlooked, questioning our assumptions, and expanding the perspectives that shape our decisions. A central mission for both of us—Marshall and Cornelia—has been helping leaders gain the insights they need to see clearly and make better decisions. In this book, we've joined forces to guide you toward becoming a panoramic leader: someone who takes into account the full spectrum of stakeholder perspectives, both inside and outside the organization, to drive smarter choices and powerful results. With that broader lens, you'll be equipped to steer your company toward greater success.

We've seen many leaders experience powerful "aha" moments as they move through this process—discovering not only how quickly they can build their panoramic leadership, but also how rewarding the journey can be. Engaging with different perspectives expands our mental maps, creates energy, and enriches our lives.

The Power of Stakeholder Perspectives

In 1987, Marshall introduced his concept of Stakeholder Centered Coaching, which tore through the business world. Before then, leadership coaching was done one-on-one and kept strictly between the coach and the leader, with the former generally being an outsider to the firm.

To create his new approach, Marshall added to the 360-degree review process, which provides leaders with input about their leadership from colleagues above, below, and around them. He'd seen that follow-up about issues raised in those reviews was often spotty, if not nonexistent. To get better results, he asked his clients to examine their 360-degree assessments and then commit to changing one or two key behaviors, as well as engage stakeholders in providing ongoing constructive feedback to them in a safe environment.

On a regular schedule, the leader follows up with those stakeholders about how they're doing in changing the behaviors they've chosen to work on. It's a uniquely effective approach that has helped some of the most successful leaders of our era achieve breakthrough success. They include Hubert Joly, who managed a dramatic turnaround as CEO of Best Buy; Alan Mulally, first as the CEO of Boeing Commercial Airplanes then as the CEO of Ford Motor Company; and Frances Hesselbein, as the CEO of the Girl Scouts of the USA.

Several years ago, Cornelia was catching up with Marshall, and she described the Leaders' Circles approach she'd created. Marshall was struck by how Cornelia's method not only aligned perfectly with his Stakeholder Centered Coaching but also extended it, updating it for coping with the brutal complexities of leadership today. He immediately brought up the idea with Cornelia to write a book together—the book you're listening to or holding in your hands.

Mike's Breakthrough

To more fully describe the power of the Leaders' Circles approach and how it helps leaders identify gaps in their strategies—the missing pieces of their maps—let's revisit Mike, the general manager.

Mike's map was very detailed when it came to local operations on the ground. He also had a strong understanding of his team members, their capabilities, how they thought, and the best ways of motivating and recognizing them. Outside the company, he understood the well-developed network of partnerships with suppliers and distributors, as well as local government officials who were vital to operations running smoothly. He was strong in his knowledge of customer segmentation, and he had good relationships with the heads of the largest customers within the country. And as he explained to the peers in his circle, he also had experience with restructuring.

Despite all that, he was still missing some important pieces.

Mike's map hadn't captured the full scope of his responsibilities to his executive team and staff. Due to his strong sense of loyalty, he believed he should be able to protect his employees from the disruptions buffeting the company. He also had a blank area regarding top management's thinking and why their changes seemed arbitrary and capricious to him. Because of these blank spaces, he felt lost.

Cornelia had chosen the participants in Mike's peer circle specifically from her one-on-one discussions with them—she knew they brought different, and at times opposing, experiences and perspectives that would help fill in the missing pieces of each other's maps. After Mike voiced the issues he was dealing with, Cornelia asked each of the peers to share their questions and offer their thoughts.

Bill, who had previously led a large division through a major restructuring, felt the same painful sense of betraying loyal team members he'd had to let go. This was one of the most difficult experiences he'd been through in his fifteen years at the top. "You'll be setting a great example for them," Bill offered, "by being a caring leader who expresses his respect and concern for them, while also carrying out the difficult work that has to be done. As they move higher up the leadership ladder, that lesson will be of great value to them."

Another peer, Emma, shared a question with Mike reflecting her own experience leading an extensive restructuring: "With as much responsibility for the company's future as you have leading its largest market, and with your unique local insights about risks to the current plan, do you believe that speaking up—stirring up some conflict if done in the right way—might help headquarters?" This question struck a chord with Mike, prompting him to consider presenting negative feedback—framed constructively—as an act of loyalty and a way of earning appreciation from top management.

At that, another participant, a CEO named Juan, chimed in. He'd been the one in his company's headquarters leading a global restructuring, and he'd made the same mistakes of not communicating enough with the leaders around him and not asking for their input. He'd been so overwhelmed with matters at hand that he just hadn't realized he was missing this vital feedback.

"Hey, Mike," he asked, "what do you think some of the leaders at headquarters are thinking, and how intentional would you say your exclusion from the decision-making process is there?"

When Mike thought about this, he understood that the alternating silence and micromanagement may not be signs of dominance but instead of indecision and misplaced belief that they had to be fully in charge.

Although he disagreed with the recent top-down instructions and the lack of transparency he perceived from top management, his deep respect for hierarchy had led him to believe that loyalty meant offering his unwavering support and acceptance. That belief kept him from voicing his concerns.

He'd felt trapped in the middle but came to see that while speaking up with constructive criticism carried some risk, his long relationship with top management meant they might well accept his feedback—if his concerns were well founded and the conditions were right. Real loyalty, he decided, meant being willing to raise those concerns.

With his map expanded, and many more options now available to him, Mike decided to share his perspective with the executive team. When he met with the CEO, his words had a powerful effect. He offered his ideas for improving their communication strategy, suggesting that many leaders beyond the headquarters walls would be open to collaborating with them on shaping this difficult restructuring.

A few days later, the top management decided to host a town hall meeting to start sharing more of their map with employees worldwide and incorporate more ideas from outside their small circle into global decision-making. Within a year, the company had completed much of its restructuring and had turned the corner.

As for Mike? He was promoted to a C-suite position.

Creating a Sphere of Understanding

One of the key goals of panoramic leadership is to create a living, breathing 3D model of the landscape affecting our business and to use it to make better decisions. You can think of this 3D model as hundreds of photos of the same place taken from every vantage point, even from below. When they're combined to intersect at a central point, they form a sphere that offers a complete picture.

Now, instead of photos of a place, imagine that you're gathering perspectives on a challenge or opportunity. The greater the range of perspectives, or the variety of your photos, the more complete the picture or your sphere of understanding becomes—and the easier it is to connect with others because you're more likely to grasp their viewpoints and the reasons behind them. The more effort you invest in incorporating different angles into your sphere, the more detailed and smoother it becomes.

A century ago, the legendary artist Picasso cocreated Cubism, which combined multiple angles of a subject in the same picture, ultimately generating a better three-dimensional understanding. According to the Tate Gallery, "By breaking objects and figures down into distinct areas—or planes—the [Cubist] artists aimed to show different viewpoints at the same time and within the same space and so suggest their three dimensional form."[11] Similarly, as a leader, it's up to you to consider the varied perspectives around you and bring them together to see a bigger whole and a more complete picture.

This is an ongoing process. The more effort you make to understand and integrate your stakeholders' experiences into your own map, the more effective your interactions with them will be and the better your decisions. And while it might seem faster to figure everything out by yourself, or with a small group of people who think just like you, ignoring others' points of view and concerns—especially if they run counter to your own—leaves you with dangerous blind spots.

We're reminded of the parable of the blind men and the elephant. The blind men have encountered an elephant for the very first time. Each of them reaches out to the animal to touch it and gain some idea of what this creature is, but each touches a different part. The man who touches the trunk thinks the elephant must resemble a snake; the man who touches the ear thinks it looks like a fan; the man who touches a leg thinks the elephant is like a tree trunk; and so on. The men argue with one another, each defending his unique perception.

The lesson is that while each of these men is correct in his assessment, none of them comprehends the big picture of what an elephant is in its entirety. The sum total of an elephant is quite different from its individual parts. Whenever we assess a situation, being right about one thing means nothing if we're blind to everything else. We must refine our own map while seeking out and understanding the perspectives of those around us.

It's not just about gathering a panorama of perspectives and saying, "Hey, I asked someone who was looking out to the north, and I asked someone who's looking south, east, and west. Now I have their perspectives." Panoramic leadership answers the question, "How do you bring those perspectives together?"

Imagine someone at the stern of your boat notices birds frantically feeding, while someone at the bow sees others flying away. Then, from the crow's nest, dark clouds are spotted in the distance. What do you make of all this? You bring these signals together and realize a storm is approaching. The birds are pre-storm feeding—they're already preparing and moving toward calmer skies. Perhaps you should follow their lead.

Cornelia coached the head of a division who's extremely driven—he's widely known to be a "tough guy"—but he also has remarkable empathy for his team members. He shared with Cornelia that it's sometimes hard for him to manage these different aspects of his personality. When these two sides clash, he has to "digest" his inner turbulence. But his career was rocketing—he regularly received positive feedback from the teams he worked with and had a long history of continuous promotions toward the top of the company.

Sometimes he found himself wondering, *Should the company follow this strategy or that strategy? No one can decide, so I'll make the decision. They'll follow my lead.* But then he would stop and ask himself, *But what about these other people? Will this decision be too much for them to handle within the time frame?*

Integrating differing stakeholder perspectives initially creates inner turbulence for this executive. Yet by analyzing multiple angles, he makes more sustainable decisions and implements them in a way that all of his different stakeholders can accept. He's well liked as a leader and successful in creating buy-in, both within and outside of his organization.

This executive came to understand a vital aspect of leadership today. There was a time when a top-down style of management could still be effective, although not optimal. But if you manage that way today, you'll be at the receiving end of resentment throughout the ranks. You also won't get the full, panoramic perspective you need to make the best decisions. Your team will be afraid to offer you their honest opinions or let you know when something is going wrong to avoid the risk of blame. And they won't tell you when they see, from the crow's nest, a storm fast approaching.

Integrating multiple views gets easier as you go. Each time you open yourself to new perspectives, the process becomes more fluid. With repetition, you begin to see more angles and a richer, fuller picture of what's possible.

Panoramic Intelligence

At its heart, panoramic intelligence is about training yourself to see through more than just your own lens. It's learning to consider the perspectives of the full range of stakeholders who affect your company—including ones who wouldn't traditionally be considered in stakeholder profiles.

It could be the person you strike up a conversation with on a plane who turns out to love a competitor's product. You can pick their brain about why. Or maybe it's taking seriously a new, niche influencer a generation younger than you. Perhaps a major shareholder presents an idea for your business that was previously nowhere on your map.

We all have some native panoramic intelligence—just as we all vary in general intelligence or emotional intelligence. The great news is that with regular commitment and practice, each of us can substantially increase our panoramic intelligence. And once you start, it quickly becomes second nature—partly because it's a joy to practice, and partly because the rewards are so immediate and lasting.

The real power comes when you move beyond simply noticing others and start to see the world through their eyes, understanding the experiences and beliefs that shape their maps. From there, it's about thoughtfully choosing which parts of other people's perspectives can expand your own, whether the insights come from someone far outside your company or from a member of your team.

Marshall reminds us that a fundamental teaching of Buddhism is impermanence (*anicca*)—nothing is permanent, and all things are subject to change, death, and renewal. The same is true for your journey as a panoramic leader. Each moment is just a snapshot. The stars move across the sky, the sun and moon rise and set, and the paths to success are ever changing.

So continuously develop your panoramic intelligence by checking in with stakeholders and adding new understanding to your map. Reach out to new people. Pay attention to unfolding events. Listen for voices you haven't heard before. Be on the lookout for allies you didn't realize you had—even those who might not always agree with you but could stand with you—and for people you can learn from. Then look beyond your current circle of allies and ask yourself: Who's not at the table? What are we not seeing? What are we not considering when we make a decision?

Too often we carry our struggles alone. But learning to share our thoughts in safe settings can be transformative—it opens the door to deeper insight, helps others truly understand us, and gives them the chance to support us more fully.

Sharing also builds trust. That's why, in Cornelia's Leaders' Circles, people begin by telling the stories of their lives—their upbringing and major life events along the way. In the next chapter, we'll do the same, sharing some of our own experiences and how they've shaped our maps, while inviting you to reflect on your own and consider how you might want to expand it.

We also share stories throughout the book of how some of the most successful leaders of recent times, in a wide range of endeavors, have expanded their maps, leading them to breakthroughs. These people include Ferran Adrià, a chef of the groundbreaking restaurant El Bulli; Alan Mulally, former CEO of Boeing Commercial Airplanes and Ford Motor Company; jazz musician Wynton Marsalis; former CEO of PepsiCo Indra Nooyi; Hubert Joly, former chairman and CEO of Best Buy; and Serena Williams, one of the greatest tennis players of all time.

A Road Map for Panoramic Success

Here's a road map for the journey you'll be taking through the heart of this book.

In chapter 2, "Take a Good Look at Your Map," we help you consider how your life experiences have shaped your own map.

Chapter 3, "Our Minds Often Mislead Us," explores the tricks our minds play on us, leading to pitfalls when we fail to adapt our maps to changing circumstances and new challenges. By cultivating awareness of these predispositions, we can navigate around them.

In chapter 4, "Mindset First," we discuss how you can adopt the right mindset for becoming a panoramic leader by igniting your curiosity and courage.

Then, in part two, we'll expand this work through the GEM Process, bringing all three lenses together in action.

In chapter 5, "Get Up Close," we show you how to reach out to stakeholders across the full breadth of your landscape.

In chapter 6, "Establish Meaningful Bonds," you'll learn how to create strong relationships with your stakeholders by first finding threads of connection with them.

Chapter 7, "Map Your Evolving Perspective," explains how to turn your discoveries and relationships into greater panoramic intelligence, and then use it to lead the way forward.

In chapter 8, "Three Principles for Making Panoramic Leadership Work," we introduce three principles for making sure people follow your lead and execute on your organization's goals.

Part three will show you how to extend your panoramic leadership, first outside of the business sphere in your own life, and then by helping others develop it themselves.

Chapter 9, "A Way of Life," shares a host of methods for applying panoramic leadership in your life, including Marshall's life plan review (LPR) process and the family plan review that Alan Mulally introduced in his own home.

Finally, in chapter 10, "Help Others Become Panoramic Leaders," we explore how to help others open their minds, expand their maps, and thrive, drawing on stories of exceptional leaders who grow others.

We're excited to have you join this journey to becoming a panoramic leader. Now, let's get started.

QUESTIONS TO CONSIDER

- Based on my life and work experiences, what are the most significant elements that make up my mental map and guide my internal GPS?
- Who are the people I could "invite up to the balcony" with me to gain fresh, panoramic perspectives on a current challenge I'm facing? What different experiences and insights might they bring?
- Reflecting on the "blind men and the elephant" story, what parts of the elephant might I be missing in my understanding of a complex situation?

- In what ways do I currently "look outward" to consider a wider range of experiences and opinions and gain a panoramic perspective for decision-making?
- When I think about a challenge I'm facing right now, whose perspectives have I already included in my "sphere of understanding," and whose perspectives might still be missing?
- To reduce the risk of perspective blindness, what events, trends, or signals in my environment deserve closer attention as I broaden my map?

CHAPTER 2

Take a Good Look at Your Map

From the moment we're born, we try to figure out how to perceive the environment around us: what's safe and what's dangerous, what we like, and what we dislike. As we get older and gain an understanding of who we are and how the world operates, this understanding forms the map we use to navigate our lives and get us where we want to go.

Our maps are continuously revised throughout our lives—sometimes by thoughtful consideration and sometimes subconsciously—by the totality of our experiences. Much like early seafaring explorers encountering unexpected territories, navigating dangerous shoals, and discovering beautiful landscapes and dramatically different lands, we make our way through life gathering new information, constantly adding insights and beliefs to our maps, and updating them as our understandings evolve. But often, after we feel we've found our sea legs, we slack off in updating our maps, and we become less conscious of the wide range of different experiences, views, beliefs, and insights that could expand our perspectives and shift our behavior.

This is a grave danger, especially in times of rapid change. Just when we think we're sailing smoothly along, confident we're on a successful trajectory, we run right into unanticipated rocky terrain or shifting winds. Many careers have been dashed to ruin in this way.

We encourage you to take time to reflect on your mental map—the formative lessons you've learned and the experiences that shaped them. Are they still helpful today? Might they be holding you back?

As you revisit the guidance you received from parents or mentors and the insights gained through both challenges and successes, reflect on how these influences are shaping your current beliefs about the path ahead. You may find that painful experiences are causing you to avoid certain options, or that past successes are leading you to overemphasize familiar skills while overlooking the need to cultivate new ones.

To help you consider the nature of your map, we're going to share our own journeys and how they've influenced our maps, hoping our stories will help you reflect on your own life experiences, which may be similar to or very different from ours. Experiences different from our own can be just as powerful as shared ones, widening our perspective and helping us draw insights from the journeys of others.

We're delighted that you're on this journey with us.

Cornelia will share her story first.

Cornelia's Journey: A Translator of Life Experiences

My life experiences led me to become a professional translator—not of languages but of people's perspectives, from one person to another, helping them decode the barriers to connecting. I learned many different "languages" that people use by living on multiple continents, watching people carefully, and working alongside them. I hardly expected my life to take me on this journey.

As a child, I was taught by my family that because I was a girl, I shouldn't take any initiative or try to do anything even slightly risky because I would likely fail and that would only cause me pain. Anytime I shared an idea or showed any ambition, I was admonished. They didn't think I was worthless; they wanted to protect me. Their mental maps—shaped by their own experiences growing up in South Korea, where women ate their meals after the men were finished and my grandmother was not allowed to learn to read—told them this was the best advice they could offer.

I was confused and troubled. Why should being a girl mean I would have to behave so differently from my brother, whom they encouraged to become a standout? While I trusted that they had my best interests at heart—and chose to do as they said, for a while—I also determined I would make up my own mind over time. I may have inherited some of that independent spirit from my grandmother, who bucked tradition and eagerly learned to read at the age of seventy.

I set off on a path of carefully observing people's behaviors, curious to understand why some people were expected to behave one way and others so differently, and then used these insights to consider the kind of person I wanted to be.

While of Korean descent, I was born and raised in Minnesota. My parents immigrated to the US and got married there, where my father began working toward his PhD at the University of Minnesota in the 1960s. After earning his degree, he took a job as an electrical engineer at Honeywell, working on the design of semiconductor chips. My mother was a talented artist who created beautiful paintings and wood carvings.

While my brother and I were two of just a few children of Asian heritage in our school, I had so much in common with the other kids that I developed a large group of friends. We loved to go swimming and to play outside—a favorite pastime of mine was skipping stones—and we indulged in ice cream whenever we got the chance.

I didn't feel "otherness." In fact, though my hair was dark brown, for a time I actually thought of myself as blond because my best friend Stacy and most of my other friends were naturally blond, thanks to their Scandinavian ancestry.

My childhood was otherwise idyllic until the age of ten, when my family moved to the bustling city of Seoul, South Korea. This was the shock of my life.

During the mid-1980s, the Korean semiconductor industry expanded rapidly, creating a pressing demand for chip designers. Samsung and other companies offered my father positions in Seoul several times. He repeatedly turned them down, until Samsung finally made him an offer that was too good to refuse. Our father promised my brother and me that we were going to "a land of great opportunity" and would be embraced by a whole world of loving relatives. The idea of leaving the home and friends I'd always known and traveling to a new country was both breathtaking and sad, but it also sounded like a dream.

On my first day at my new school in Seoul, during a break between classes, I approached a group of girls I'd met in class to say hello. As I walked toward them, they turned their backs to me and formed a tight circle, blocking me out. I was confused. Then mortified. I felt physically sick and almost dizzy. No one had ever treated me so rudely before, and I had no idea why they were purposefully making me feel so excluded. My face burned with embarrassment as I walked away.

During lunch, when I tried to sit down with some other classmates, one girl turned toward me and said in a nasty voice, "Don't sit here!" I impulsively turned around to see who she was talking to so disparagingly before I was stung by the realization that she was talking to *me*. I felt my breath grow short and my body felt numb. Looking around the room, I saw everyone chatting away with their friends, and I felt as if I didn't exist. As I turned to leave the cafeteria, my legs moved robotically. I headed to the library to read alone, aching to be with my friends back home in Minnesota.

Used to being surrounded by friends, I felt a deep loneliness, and that moment imprinted on my mental map the value of reaching out to other kids I saw sitting by themselves. In the future, I'd walk over and strike up a conversation in case they'd appreciate the company.

The great irony was that in Seoul, while I looked like the people around me, I felt so different, so out of place. I didn't know how to *be* Korean, and my classmates and the relatives who were supposedly eager to spend time with me were mystified and annoyed by my behavior. One uncle admonished me for being too bold and assertive. "You look Korean, but you're not acting Korean."

I was confused about how I could fit in better. Then one day I watched a TV interview with an actress who spoke about being a single mother and how she felt loneliness, sadness, and frustration. What struck me was when she described how these feelings enabled her to more authentically portray characters in her movies. Just as she needed to understand the characters she portrayed, I realized that if I wanted to bond with people, I needed to *understand them*—and that was the start of a lifelong quest to learn about how others think and how to connect with them.

I began to immerse myself in the local Korean culture, and my life transformed. Each new experience was a gift—not all of them fun, but always enriching, and something to be appreciated and to learn from. While my family members had said I'd be hurt if I asserted myself, I decided I was going to do just that.

I started making friends, and I didn't limit myself to one group, or even to kids my own age. Within a few years of moving to Seoul, I was the only middle schooler chosen for a role in the high school musical.

I remember singing a duet onstage under the hot lights, looking out at the theater filled with most of the student body, and thinking about how many of them I could call a friend. I'd been accepted by a wide variety of groups because I'd succeeded in understanding them and in helping them understand me. I'd achieved what I'd thought, on that first day of school, was out of reach—the joy of acceptance.

But I was about to be confronted by another life-changing challenge.

My brother, who was two years ahead of me at school, was brilliant at mathematics, and while we were still living in Seoul, he was accepted to Phillips Exeter Academy, a co-ed boarding school in New Hampshire. While I attended a tour of the school with my family, I learned about opportunities there to meet people from around the world and all the different sports the school offered. Right then and there, I made it my mission to follow in my brother's footsteps.

When I told my parents I wanted to apply, they said, "Absolutely not! You're a girl!" But after years of defying those early childhood instructions, my map had already changed. I insisted on applying. My parents finally relented, but they told me, "You're not going to get in, and that'll be the end of the story. Do you understand?"

"Okay. I understand." If I didn't get in, I wouldn't mention it again.

I waited anxiously for months. Then a letter from Exeter arrived and I was in!

My parents threw no celebration for me. My father said nothing about it, at least not to me. I left my acceptance letter on the kitchen table for them to contemplate. Eventually, they reluctantly agreed to let me attend.

I was hesitant to share the news with my classmates, but when I finally told them, they organized a surprise going-away party for me. The same people who had shut me out of their circle at the beginning of my time in Seoul now told me how much they would miss me. We had shared an important part of our lives together, and I realized I'd etched indelible experiences of friendship in my memory.

Leaving Seoul was bittersweet. It had become home, and the people who lived there became part of my identity. My friends, my memories of discovering a new city and a new way of being, and learning to thrive there were all part of my map.

Once at Exeter, I did meet people from all over the world. And the American culture was familiar. But life at a boarding school was not, requiring new adjustments—for instance, to Saturday classes and strict curfews. After three years of boarding school life, I jumped at the opportunity to spend my final year of high school studying abroad in Barcelona, Spain. Because I was new to the country and a young student, I wanted to connect with everybody I met. Again, I bonded with a wide range of people, this time from some of the highest echelons of society to the poorest, through a theater group I started for homeless children.

In each new culture I experienced, I was perceived as different from those around me, and that taught me to translate my experiences and my views for people so that they could understand me. In return, they shared their own experiences and views with me. Feeling comfortable opening up about myself and finding ways to build bridges of understanding with people became an important part of my map.

After high school, I attended Georgetown University in Washington, DC. There I had the uniquely humbling experience of gaining a front-row seat in highly influential centers of power, working with top-level officials in government, international organizations, and business. I spent an eye-opening summer interning in the office of the United Nations Special Assistant to the High Commissioner for Human Rights. Due to a lack of space in the interns' office, my desk was located in the commissioner's offices for a week! This inconvenience for the high commissioner and his team turned into a rare opportunity for me.

At first, conscious of the gulf between my limited experience and that of the leaders in the room, I felt completely out of place, like I had wandered into a world that operated far above my head. I stayed quiet, worried that speaking up would reveal how little I knew. Instead, I devoted myself to listening closely—to world leaders in conversation with one another and their teams—and to observing how they treated each other.

What I learned surprised me.

They weren't superhuman, all-wise, or all-knowing. They were relatable. They were just smart, experienced human beings with a great amount of responsibility. I even started to feel a certain familiarity with them. This familiarity and growing comfort with world leaders would be crucial for me in the coming months.

Back during my first month of college, I launched a program to help women from around the world start their own companies through a youth business organization called AIESEC (Association Internationale des Étudiants en Sciences Économiques et Commerciales). I was motivated by my time in Seoul, where I had watched female family friends struggle to find corporate jobs. Others and I believed young women could gain experience in the business world by starting and running their own companies. And so I reached out to corporate CEOs, finance executives, and other key business leaders, asking them to serve as mentors for these entrepreneurs. Meeting with executives on the top floors of shiny corporate buildings as a college freshman, dressed in my most professional suit, I was struck by how receptive they were to our program. We ultimately received support not just from these executives but also from media representatives, publishers, nonprofit leaders, and government officials.

Growing this program led to my selection as a youth speaker at a major United Nations conference where the secretary-general invited me to join meetings with heads of state and senior government officials. In those rooms, global leaders asked for my candid advice on a variety of pressing issues affecting their countries and citizens. For example, I remember that a leader across the room asked for my opinion on how to boost economic growth in a sustainable way.

For a split second, I froze—my mind racing. What could I possibly say to contribute?

Then I thought back to my own journey: living across three continents, in places that had invested heavily in education and others that had not. Through my relationships with people at the very top of society and those struggling at the bottom, I saw that, although not the only factor, education made an enormous difference. Gathering my courage, I shared some of my experience and suggested that one of the pillars of development should be education, because it grows the economy from the ground up by investing in the workforce. To my surprise, the room leaned in, nodding as I spoke.

The minister looked at me and said he would do exactly that.

Relief washed over me—quickly followed by a surprising surge of joy. I'd shared something that helped them.

I also realized I'd learned the language of leaders well enough to share my insights in terms they could understand. I called these *microtranslations*—taking an idea or lesson from one context and adapting it to another so people could apply it in a new way. So often, our best ideas come from entirely different settings. By adopting the role of translator, I found I could help people understand and connect with me, even if we were very different from one another. I learned from this experience not to hesitate to reach out and connect with anyone.

A few months later, I began an internship at the White House, working in the office of the first lady of the United States. One morning, as we stood on the lawn in the warm spring sunshine, I felt excited and humbled to have this one-on-one time with the first lady. She then surprised me by asking for my opinion on several matters unfolding in her office. I was startled to hear myself answering each of her questions in clear, coherent sentences, despite how nervous I felt.

She was silent for what felt like a very long moment, and I began to wonder if I'd said the wrong thing. Then she smiled, said, "Thank you, that's very helpful," and extended her hand to shake mine. I was thrilled.

That moment, and others like it, showed me a different side of leadership. I realized how challenging it is for leaders at the top of organizations to gather all the information they need to make good decisions—which is why some sought out different viewpoints at every opportunity, even from me. Despite my youth, by sharing my observations I could fill in empty areas of their mental maps, broadening their view and helping them understand more. In my own small way, I helped expand the panorama of perspectives they considered—even those beyond their usual circles—supporting them in making better decisions.

After graduating from university and earning my master's degree, I joined the world of private equity investment, an experience that gave me a wider, more detailed perspective on business across North America, Asia, and Europe. One meeting with senior bank leaders left a particular mark on me.

I'd presented some of my firm's asset valuations, and the bank leaders immediately responded with annoyed defensiveness. For a moment, I worried the conversation would stall. But as I listened more closely, I realized our perspectives overlapped far more than I first thought—we were simply using different languages to describe the same reality. Years of observing people in different situations had taught me to notice those patterns, to decode contrasting perspectives and translate them into common ground. Once I highlighted our broad areas of agreement, the tension eased, and we found a way forward.

That moment showed me something essential: Leadership isn't just about offering your own ideas. It's about bringing people together so they can learn from one another.

For the last thirty years, as I've worked closely with CEOs and top leaders around the globe, I've been guided by a belief formed through my experiences: There is something to learn from *everyone*. Living out this belief, I immersed myself in learning from all kinds of people—including taxi drivers and people I met on airplanes—to hear their stories and to learn their priorities, their motivations, and their dreams. No matter how different from me someone seemed at first, there was always something we shared—a thread that we could build on.

When I moved to Geneva, Switzerland, and discovered that the private equity industry was still in its infancy there, I decided to change careers. For a time, I felt lost again, almost as lost as I'd been when I moved to Seoul as a ten-year-old. To find my way, I started interviewing leaders of all sorts, eventually speaking to more than one hundred of them from all around the world. One question I asked each of them was, "What does it take to succeed?" Over and over, they responded with a version of, "You need trusted thought partners, because it's too lonely to go it alone."

This was when I found my North Star—or my Southern Cross for readers in the southern hemisphere—the guiding sense of purpose that showed me how to combine all of the parts of my map: I would bring leaders together so that they could learn from each other. Selecting people to join Leaders' Circles, getting to know them, and moderating their discussions has been the most exciting and rewarding work of my entire career.

Next, Marshall.

Marshall's Journey: From Valley Station to the World Stage

I'm from a small town called Valley Station, Kentucky, which was somewhat lost in time. During my first four years of elementary school, we had a primitive outhouse for our bathroom because the building had no indoor plumbing. Funding for education was lean, and my high school was ranked second from the very bottom in Kentucky in academic achievement. And at the time, Kentucky was ranked near the bottom in academic achievement for the entire United States.

My father, Bill, owned a gas station, and our house was located between the station and a bar, which was a rowdy place. Fights regularly broke out, often involving soldiers from nearby Fort Knox. The street in front of our house—the Dixie Highway—was nicknamed the "Dixie Dieway" because it was the scene of so many deadly car wrecks. I can remember at least nine deaths on the Dieway when I was growing up.

My mother, Margaret, went to college for two years, which was very unusual for women in my neighborhood, and for some years, she was a primary school teacher. But my father thought women with children should not work outside the home, and one of the bad outcomes from that decision was that we became very poor. The good news was that my mother devoted all her schoolteacher energy to just one student: *me*. I learned how to add, subtract, multiply, and divide before I went to elementary school.

It probably won't surprise you to learn that after my first day of school I concluded I must be the smartest person who ever lived. What might surprise you is that later in my academic career, when I was in high school, I was not a great achiever. In fact, I was something of a troublemaker. When I was fourteen, I earned the honor of being the first in my class to be detained by the police, for disorderly conduct. The same year, I was kicked out of my church.

I was raised as a Southern Baptist. One day I asked my Sunday school teacher why everyone who wasn't a Southern Baptist—Muslims, Jews, Buddhists, Hindus, and even Catholics and those in other Christian denominations—was destined to go to hell. My church leaders decided I had an attitude problem. Looking back, I don't think I was being snarky; I was honestly curious why we were the only ones chosen to go to heaven.

Thankfully, that year I also had the great fortune of going to work for Dennis Mudd, a roofer who was replacing some shingles on the roof of our house, which had started leaking during a rainstorm. My dad thought maybe he could save some money if I helped Dennis, so I became Mr. Mudd's junior assistant roofer. Putting on a new roof was very hard work in the hot and humid Kentucky summer, one of the hardest jobs I've ever had. Even though we started early in the day to beat the heat, I was a tired, sweaty mess at the end of each workday.

We worked together for the better part of a week, and throughout it all, Dennis Mudd was very kind to me. He did his best to teach me all about roofing—he wanted his junior assistant roofer to know how to do quality work. After we were done, he went to talk to my father.

"Bill, I want you to inspect the roof," he said. "If that roof is of high quality, pay me. And if it's not of high quality, it's all free."

I looked at Dennis and I thought to myself, *This man is poor, but he is not cheap. He has integrity.* And at that very moment, as a fourteen-year-old boy, I decided I wanted to be just like Dennis Mudd when I grew up. I wanted to have the same courage to be able to stand up and say that I believe in what I am doing.

I followed Dennis's lead when I became an executive coach and decided to tell clients that I wouldn't bill them if, after we'd worked together, they didn't improve. This didn't take as much courage as Dennis had shown, because he really needed the money, whereas I had a good financial cushion. And in fact, this practice has been hugely rewarding, because I know when I'm paid that I've helped my clients achieve an important breakthrough in their lives.

Another major life lesson I learned was drummed into me by my mother. Although I was not a motivated student in high school, she was determined that I would go to college. I wasn't so sure that was the right path for me, but she constantly impressed on me, "You *will* go to college." I can clearly see now that she couldn't bear the idea of seeing me pumping gas and doing oil changes at my father's gas station for the rest of my life. And if I hadn't gone to college, that could have very well been my fate.

To help guard against that possibility, or that I might decide to go into a trade instead, she would tell me, "You have no mechanical skills, and you will *never* have any mechanical skills." My father got on the bandwagon. Despite owning a gas station, he never encouraged me to learn about cars or any other mechanical things.

My parents knew me well. When I turned eighteen, I took a US Army aptitude test—thinking that instead of going to college I might join the military. Guess where I scored for my mechanical skills? In the bottom 2 percent for the entire United States. Now it was official: My mother was right, and I would head to college.

Despite my lackluster high school performance, I was fortunate enough to earn high scores on the Scholastic Aptitude Test, which enabled me to earn a scholarship. I enrolled as an undergraduate at Rose-Hulman Institute of Technology in Terre Haute, Indiana—a little more than three hours by car from my home in Valley Station. Rose-Hulman is a wonderful school, and it's easy to see why, for twenty-six consecutive years, it has been ranked by *U.S. News & World Report* as the number one small engineering school in the United States. I, however, continued my less-than-stellar academic career while I was there. I made five Ds and was lucky to graduate.

But my mother's belief in the value of higher learning had sunk in, and combined with my near-perfect GMAT score, I received a scholarship to pursue an MBA from the Kelley School of Business at Indiana University. I went on to earn a PhD from the University of California, Los Angeles (UCLA) Anderson School of Management, which instilled a love for my chosen field, organizational behavior. Ultimately, my mother's influence had opened my eyes to the joy of education, and my transformation invested in me the conviction that we can all change our behaviors and become more effective in our personal and professional lives. That drew me to the work of coaching. It also drove me to pursue a life of continuous learning and growth, both personally and professionally.

When I received an honorary PhD in engineering from Rose-Hulman in 2023, I was invited to give the 145th commencement address. Standing before the students, I enjoyed sharing my own early struggles in college. So imagine the students' surprise when I told them that many years earlier, I had graduated by the skin of my teeth. That was a great opportunity to send a message about life's vast possibilities. At the end, I led the student body in a standing ovation for the bottom half of the class. I wanted to underscore that they were full of promise.

Another crucial experience that contributed to my map came from my time in Los Angeles working on my PhD. I joined up with some encounter groups, which provided the seed for my eventual work in coaching. Encounter groups—Esalen, EST, T-groups, and more—became a movement in the sixties, and they were popular through the seventies and well into the eighties. The idea is for participants in a group, guided by a facilitator, to share emotional reactions (anger, fear, warmth, envy) to others' actions and statements. By focusing on emotions rather than judgments, participants learn how their communication triggers emotional responses in others.

I participated in one group two days a week for eight hours each day. During that time, we would switch roles. I led the group for two hours, then observed the group for two hours, then was actually in the group for two hours, then critiqued the group for the last two hours. This went on for five months. Let me tell you—we had some wild sessions! Many insults were hurled around, plenty of egos were bruised, and gallons of tears were shed. However, these sessions taught me three valuable lessons that I carried with me into my coaching work.

First, unstructured environments make people very anxious. People prefer having structure in their lives, whether at work or in their personal lives. Routines rule.

Second, the kind of unvarnished honesty that we practiced in our encounter groups is not usually appreciated in a business context.

Finally, I learned that as difficult as it may be to hear honest feedback, receiving it is invaluable to one's personal growth.

At work, getting honest feedback and providing it to others are critical to your success. This process provides you with the information you need to improve your performance, enhance your relationships, and thereby achieve your goals. Particularly constructive is offering what I call "feedforward," which means focusing on future-oriented suggestions for improvement rather than dwelling on past mistakes.

All of these experiences combined to inspire me to dedicate my career to helping leaders achieve positive, lasting change in behavior for themselves, their teams, and their organizations. In the course of my coaching, I learned the power of storytelling as a tool for connecting with others. In particular, sharing our personal stories helps build empathy between people and conveys aspects of our personalities, viewpoints, and values that we often don't share in our business lives—and even in our personal lives with many of our acquaintances. While I generally keep my personal life private, I've been happy to relate these formative experiences to you as part of our mission in this book to encourage you to examine your own such experiences and how they've shaped your map.

The concept of earning your life, as I've discussed in my teachings, is about making a meaningful difference, and I hope that my life story—and this book—will inspire you to do just that.

Updating Your Map as the World Changes

With the world changing so quickly, if we want to succeed, we have no choice but to change with it. This is hard for many reasons, as we'll explore in the pages ahead. One of them is that we prefer the way things have been—the world we've become comfortable with.

Cornelia compares this to the emotions she used to feel when she visited the cities where she'd once lived and saw how much they'd changed. Whole new parts of Seoul were built as South Korea prospered. In Barcelona, the Poblenou neighborhood, among others, had been transformed into a thriving new community with new housing, parks, galleries, restaurants, and shops. That was wonderful to see, but Cornelia also felt an intense sense of loss. She had so many fond memories of these places and the experiences she'd enjoyed there—as it was before.

But after adjusting to the shock of so much change, Cornelia realized that much had actually remained the same from when she lived in those places, and she could still enjoy those aspects of the cities while appreciating how they were transforming. She came to see cities not as fixed in time but as growing communities that must always be taking advantage of new opportunities for growth. This is what makes them vibrant and resilient.

The same is true of our mental maps. Like evolving cities, they need constant updating. As with beautiful old sections of Seoul and

Barcelona, we don't have to toss out parts of our maps that are valuable to us. But we should retire what's outdated and expand into new territory. Early experiences can imprint beliefs that, when revisited later, conflict with where we're headed. By seeking new perspectives and testing those beliefs, we keep what works, let go of what doesn't, and widen our panorama of possibilities through our expanded maps.

The Three Lenses of Panoramic Leadership

Taken as a whole, our maps can only ever be as accurate as the lenses we use to see and interpret the world around us. If our maps help us chart this landscape, our lenses determine how sharply we perceive it. They color how we interpret what we learn, how we adapt our maps, and how we share our insights with our stakeholders.

If you look back at the stories we've shared, you may notice a pattern. Each of us engaged in inner work, examining the experiences and assumptions that shaped us. We looked outward, learning from changing environments and from the people around us. And we translated our experiences so others could understand them, while allowing their perspectives to broaden our own. In doing so, we were already using three distinct lenses.

These three lenses—inner, outer, and relational—allow us to understand the world more fully and lead more effectively. The inner lens, through self-reflection, helps us recognize our perceptions, assumptions, and fears. The outer lens widens our view through interaction with stakeholders, taking in the systems, perspectives, and shifting conditions that define the world around us.

The relational lens is different. It is a living prism positioned between our inner map and the outer world. It transforms the experiences and perspectives—the light—we take in from the outside and casts a spectrum of insight onto our map. That refracted light helps us refine our map, clarifying patterns and revealing connections we could not see alone.

But the flow of light doesn't stop there. The relational lens gathers the insights we develop internally and shines that light back outward to our stakeholders through our outer lens, expressed in dialogue and leadership. In this way, the prism of the relational lens keeps the exchange between our inner map and the outer environment alive.

This continuous refraction of insight—taking in light and returning it transformed—is what distinguishes panoramic leaders. Their insight is not a private possession; it is shared light. They do not merely absorb understanding from all sides; they refract it back outward toward their stakeholders, shaping conversations and aligning teams.

Together, these three lenses enable leaders to create more accurate maps, see patterns others miss, stay connected to their stakeholders, and act with clarity even amid complexity. This integration is where panoramic leadership is born, allowing us to make better decisions, act wisely, and help others see more together.

THE THREE LENSES OF PANORAMIC LEADERSHIP

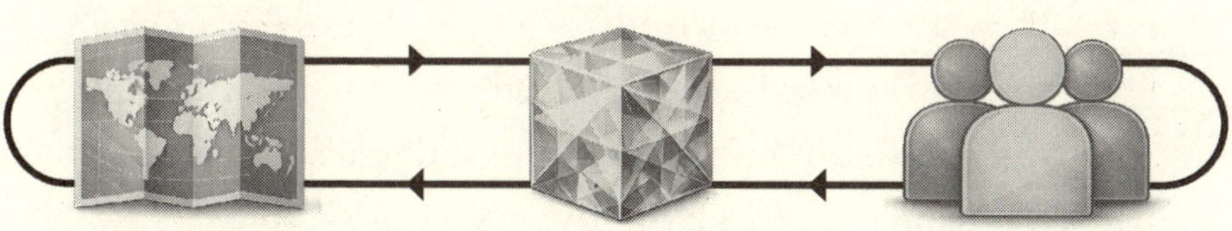

INNER LENS

How I see myself and regulate my internal map

RELATIONAL LENS

How we create insight by combining perspectives

OUTER LENS

How we engage the wider stakeholder system

We'll be revisiting these lenses throughout the coming chapters. In the next two chapters, we'll explore how our inner lens affects how we see the world through our outer lens. Then in part two, we'll expand this work through the GEM Process, bringing all three lenses together in action.

Before we dive into the journey, take a moment to assess what your map looks like now—how it reflects the details of your life and influences how you navigate your current environment.

QUESTIONS TO CONSIDER

- What lessons from my childhood experiences are part of my personal map? How have those lessons shaped my life?
- How can I learn from others' experiences and turn those insights into meaningful additions to my own map?
- What limiting beliefs formed by past encounters might make it harder for me to expand my worldview?
- How can I translate my experiences so that other people who see the world differently can understand them?
- How do the insights from each of my lenses expand or reshape the map I'm using to lead?
- In what ways have I added insights and beliefs to my map throughout my life? How have those beliefs evolved?

CHAPTER 3

Our Minds Often Mislead Us

Humans have created maps since at least the late Paleolithic period (the Old Stone Age). One early example is an engraving on a mammoth tusk from about twenty-five thousand years ago, found in the Czech Republic, which consists of markings interpreted as a mountain, a river, valleys, and trails near a settlement.

The technology of mapmaking has constantly evolved, as have the kinds of features depicted. Yet regardless of the technology, maps have always been tailored to their times and the needs of their users—from Ptolemy's ancient grids of latitude and longitude drawn across the globe to the cycling maps that emerged in the wake of the late nineteenth-century bicycle craze in France, which highlighted changes in elevation so cyclists knew where the tough going would be.[1]

According to historians, European maps from earlier centuries didn't always include roads. Instead, they marked the way from one village or town to another with references to other settlements along the way and to natural features, such as streams or stands of trees. Molly Taylor-Poleskey, Harvard map librarian and the curator of "Rivers & Roads: The Art of Getting There," a Harvard Library exhibit displaying Parisian bicycling maps and other examples of mapmaking across cultures, stresses, "Mapmakers are always selective."[2] In truth, maps have never been entirely objective depictions but rather have been drawn through the subjective perspective of their makers. What they believed was important was included, with much else left out.

So, too, are our mental maps subjective, and we're in great danger of misreading the terrain we're mapping if we don't continuously get input from others. If we're unwilling to question whether the maps we've created still reflect the changing world around us, we miss the signs in our environment foreshadowing changes coming at us—and the challenges and opportunities they present.

One key problem is that our comfort with our maps lulls us into relying too much on them and going on autopilot.

Assuming We Know the Way

These days, commercial airline pilots fly planes largely on autopilot. Before takeoff, they program the flight plan in the system and it automatically guides the airplane, generally until landing. This has proven extremely safe, but that's because pilots continuously monitor the course, ready to adjust flight parameters including altitude and speed if necessary.

Human brains have a kind of "autopilot" too. It often serves us well—but it only works when the environment is stable. If you commute to work, you probably leave your home at about the same time every workday and take the same route—whether in a car, subway, or train. Say you're driving and you keep an eye on the speedometer and the road ahead. You might pride yourself on being a superior driver because you also regularly look farther down the road and check your rearview mirror frequently. But some of the time, you may be on autopilot, caught up in listening to music.

You can still get to work safely because you're driving on familiar roads, and you and the other drivers generally follow the rules. It's an extremely prescriptive experience. Stay between the lines, switch on your turn signal when you want to move from one lane to another, and keep some distance from the car in front of you. These rules and norms are so deeply ingrained in us that we follow them without much conscious thought. Except for those rare times when something out of the ordinary happens, such as a snowstorm or sudden downpour that makes the roads dangerously slick.

Our minds love going on autopilot—it saves time and conserves energy by sparing us the burden of rethinking much of what we do. Just in terms of energy, Dr. Marcus Raichle, neurologist and professor of medicine at the Washington University School of Medicine in St. Louis, reports that "as an energy consumer, the brain is the most expensive organ we carry around with us."[3] While the average human brain takes up about 2 percent of a person's body weight, it consumes around 20 percent of oxygen and calories—more than any other organ.[4]

So it makes sense that our minds push us to autopilot whenever possible—we burn fewer calories, conserving energy for when we really need it to focus and think deeply.

Autopilot can work on familiar roads, but today's business landscape is anything but familiar. Standards, norms, and rules are changing for industries around the world. We're facing new hazards in our environment. Yet so many of us are still driving as if we're on safe, familiar roads and can depend on others to respect the rules. In reality, we're in uncharted territory.

As Dorie Clark reminds us in *The Long Game*, "No matter how good you are, you can't win any game by doing the same thing all the time."[5] Sustained success requires continual adjustment—lifting your gaze, testing new approaches, and staying responsive to the changing landscape around you. If you're not constantly scanning from side to side as well as in front and behind—getting inputs from every direction—you'll be left with blind spots, and you could be vulnerable to an accident waiting to happen.

A couple years ago, we were approached with an opportunity to coach the new CEO of a large, multinational corporation with a name you would instantly recognize. Before accepting this promotion, he'd accumulated a long list of accomplishments, including an overflowing stack of accolades from his previous organizations and crucial C-suite experience guiding his company through some very challenging transitions.

This CEO, who exuded warmth, seemingly checked all the boxes. He was smart and gave credit to others where credit was due. He wasn't afraid to apologize, and kept his emotions in check during some very tough situations, reliably maintaining his cool. What's more, he had all the initiative anyone could ever want, and he was a big-picture thinker, moving the company forward into new business areas while strengthening the current ones.

Although we ended up deciding not to work with this CEO, from our conversations with him, we know he believed he was doing a good job. Yet, before he was able to celebrate his first anniversary, the board asked him to step down. Why?

He'd engaged only a handful of stakeholders for their perspectives on the business. He was so busy moving forward that he failed to consult some members of his own C-suite about his plans. Because he never sought their input, he didn't know about an issue that had grown into a serious financial risk for the company. He also didn't build meaningful connections with most of the board members. They grew frustrated that he hadn't seriously considered their input, and some were alarmed by the escalating problem in one of the company's divisions.

The board had become deeply displeased with him, but he missed the cues of his impending dismissal. He was completely blindsided when he was shown the door.

In fact, we're seeing a strong trend of leadership not working out. A record number of CEOs left their roles for the second consecutive year in 2025—up 16 percent from the prior year and 21 percent above the eight-year average.[6] This story of the CEO who was shocked by his sudden dismissal highlights a key lesson: When we rely too heavily on autopilot—operating only from our own map—and fail to connect with our panorama of stakeholders, we stop updating our view of the landscape. And in a rapidly changing world, this can quickly lead to disaster.

Taking Shortcuts

The brain tends to simplify, make assumptions, and rely on generalizations—all part of our built-in autopilot guidance systems. We rely on these various thinking shortcuts even more when we're contending with overwhelming uncertainty. These shortcuts help us to function, but they can also create blind spots and biases in our maps, as well as complacency and overconfidence in what we know, all of which can lead to catastrophic decision-making.

One of the shortcuts our brains resort to when confronting uncertainty is forcing the unknown into something familiar, more easily enabling us to operate on autopilot. Generalization is one way we do this.

Research conducted by psychology professor Alexander Todorov and then-student researcher Janine Willis found that people form first impressions about someone they just met literally in an instant—a tenth of a second—based solely on facial characteristics. And the judgments we make aren't just trivial ones, such as about someone's haircut. We make snap judgments about a person's character—their trustworthiness, competence, and aggressiveness.[7]

Todorov shares that we can't really rely on these impressions to be correct. "Given that impressions of the same person vary across different images, they can hardly be accurate assessments of the person's character."[8]

He points out that impressions drawn from images are unreliable, since they capture only a single moment in time and therefore offer little basis for judging a person's true character. Even when an observer accurately identifies emotions such as anxiety, irritation, or calmness, those fleeting expressions reveal only a temporary state rather than enduring qualities.

This is just one of many types of bias our minds are prone to, which can lead us to misread people, situations, the nature of challenges, and even the best options for addressing them.

The Pull of the Immediate and the Familiar

When faced with ambiguity, another type of bias we often fall prey to is short-term bias—a tendency to favor quick solutions over longer-term strategies. It can lead to long-term problems, such as failing systems that weren't upgraded when they should have been.

So, why do we keep focusing on the short term? One reason is the stress of uncertainty, which often increases the further out we project. Immediate actions or quick fixes—which may not be fixes at all—can feel safer and more within our control, even if they undermine better long-term solutions. This pattern reinforces what's known as hyperbolic discounting, a cognitive bias that leads us to place higher value on quick rewards over greater future gain.[9] We may also give greater weight to negative events in our lives than positive ones, a tendency known as negativity bias.[10] As a result, we might pay more attention to the costs or risks of making a change than to its potential benefits.

With volatility all around us, it can feel easier to ignore change altogether. When we don't take emerging threats seriously enough, we might not even consider longer-term solutions or see the potential cost of inaction. Confirmation bias can compound this problem, drawing our attention to what we want to see and discounting what we don't, including important warning signs. In *Decisive*, authors Chip Heath and Dan Heath name confirmation bias as one of the four villains of decision-making: "When we want something to be true, we will spotlight the things that support it, and then, when we draw conclusions from those spotlighted scenes, we'll congratulate ourselves on a reasoned decision."[11]

All of these cognitive biases mean that when the future feels uncertain, we're inclined to gravitate toward what's immediate, familiar, and close at hand. This tendency doesn't just shape how we navigate change—it also affects whose voices and perspectives we pay attention to. Leaders who overlook more distant stakeholders or refuse to engage with them—to listen and understand them—risk missing crucial signals that could shape important decisions. Let's see how that played out at Blockbuster, Inc.

The classic riches-to-rags story of Blockbuster is well known, as is its missed chance to buy its upstart competitor, Netflix, for $50 million. Less well known, though, is another missed opportunity by then CEO John Antioco. He waited too long to engage with a powerful stakeholder who, though distant in his mind, had suddenly emerged as a force to be reckoned with: activist investor Carl Icahn.

At the time, Blockbuster was a video-rental behemoth with more than nine thousand stores across the globe and billions of dollars in annual revenue. In 2004, Icahn, famous for acquiring significant ownership stakes in companies and pressuring management for strategic changes, turned his attention to Blockbuster. By 2005, he'd acquired almost 10 percent of the company's stock and phoned Antioco with a series of requests, which included extending the deadline for shareholders to nominate directors ahead of the upcoming annual meeting. Icahn argued that "the additional time would be used to explore methods of enhancing shareholder value" that each of them would find acceptable.[12]

As Antioco shared in an article he wrote for the *Harvard Business Review,* "It was a complete surprise. I knew, of course, that Icahn was an 'activist shareholder,' but I had no idea why he might be calling."[13] Despite his admitted lack of information or awareness, he didn't meet with Icahn to get up close to him and defuse the situation or try to understand the map he was using to navigate.

Instead, Antioco wrote Icahn the next day and rejected all of his requests.

The following day, Icahn wrote Antioco, recalling his earlier words that "the postponement might have given us a small window to discuss our differences,"[14] and then launched a proxy fight—and won. It was only *after* Icahn's victory in May 2005 that Antioco met him face-to-face for the first time.

By starting off in conflict with Icahn, Antioco only fueled tensions, which grew far worse. Icahn's efforts to oust the CEO eventually succeeded when Antioco stepped down in July 2007. Looking back, Antioco admitted: "I probably should have met with Carl earlier, before the proxy fight, to lay out what we were doing and why."[15] Instead, focused on the short term and the familiar, he realized too late that even an emerging stakeholder needed to be engaged and convinced of his strategy and decisions.

If we want to succeed in this complex, uncertain world, we must engage with both the stakeholders closest to us and those who seem distant or unfamiliar, listening to their perspectives and, when appropriate, weaving them into our own maps—even when it feels uncomfortable or inconvenient.

The Threat Responses

Feeling fear in the midst of change and uncertainty is entirely understandable—and can, in fact, be a natural adaptive response for us as human beings. Fear itself is not a bad thing. When Cornelia's son was a toddler, he didn't have enough fear of fire, which led him to try to grab a candle flame. Ouch!

The problem is that fear can overstimulate our classic fight-flight-freeze behaviors, each of which can lead to disaster.

Fight. This is an active, often aggressive response to change perceived as a threat. We express a desire to neutralize the source of change, whether it's people, ideas, situations, or environments.

A top executive at a software as a service (SaaS) company was asked by her CEO to hire an expert in artificial intelligence, as the capabilities of AI were disrupting the SaaS market. New AI-powered services offered functionality that competed with this company's products—capabilities that the company's existing products couldn't match. The executive told us: "I don't need expertise on disruption. *I am* the disruptor." It was true that more than a decade earlier, as a start-up, the company had disrupted many of the offerings of top software companies, especially when they were sold on disks and CD-ROMs.

But now, the software world was changing so quickly that features that had previously taken months to build were being offered in days. Some large corporations were also building their own customized software instead of subscribing to SaaS products. The SaaS disruptors were now becoming disrupted themselves by new AI-based products.

The top executive complied and hired an employee from an AI-based company. But then she pushed back. Instead of embracing the new opportunities that the AI expert could open up to the company, she fought against these opportunities and dismissed the new employee—a decision that turned out to be a big mistake. Several established clients left and potential new ones repeatedly rejected the firm because, unsurprisingly, they expected AI capabilities to be a given in the modern software industry.

Flight. Too often, we run away from change in the hope of avoiding it, mainly by disregarding our own need to adapt in response to evolving circumstances and instead gravitating toward familiar territory.

Years ago, at a boutique asset management firm, the management committee advised the COO to start operations in Asia to capitalize on high-growth markets and boost global returns. The economies of many Asian markets were booming, creating an attractive opportunity. But this leader felt overwhelmed by the task, especially as he was planning to announce his retirement in just three years.

He cited many reasons for not moving to Asia. "It would take too long to get returns on our investment," he said. "I don't know if we'd open an office or just send one or two people. Overall, I think we should open another office in Europe, where we already have relationships and traction." When asked how much work he'd done to investigate the feasibility of expanding operations into Asia, he admitted he'd asked two people to look into it but he hadn't really done anything with the reports.

The COO avoided engagement with an important part of the evolving global economy and ignored the growing need to jump into what he saw as unknown and potentially perilous territory. Instead, he decided to do more of what was already familiar, which was expanding operations in Europe without getting up close to the change in Asia and dealing with it head-on.

Freeze. Sometimes, we recognize the change in front of us—and may even see the need to adapt—but find ourselves too paralyzed to move forward. We get stuck, delaying decisions and actions that need to happen.

Freezing can be a problem when designing, developing, and launching new products. What may appear to be productive activity is sometimes just "analysis paralysis," or overanalyzing to the point that it keeps us from making a choice or taking action. In some cases, excessive prototyping and market testing are simply forms of denial that the right option is to drop the effort.

For a decade, Apple spent an average of $1 billion a year on the development of a fully autonomous car that was unlike any other on the road. According to a report, "The company toiled away on at least five different major designs, drove prototype self-driving systems for more than a million miles, hired engineers and designers only to lay them off, and weighed partnerships or acquisitions with Tesla, Mercedes-Benz, BMW, Volkswagen and McLaren Automotive, among others."[16]

After ten years of work on the project and about a fifth of the company's R&D budget when the project started—more than $10 billion—sunk into it, in February 2024, Apple pulled the plug on its car. According to Bloomberg, the failure wasn't just due to the difficulty of the technology. It was also a failure by company leadership to choose one path to follow. They were stuck on autopilot, unable to take control. As one executive who worked on the car put it, "The big arc was poor leadership that let the program linger, while everyone else in Apple was cringing."[17]

A recent study by HSBC found that 32 percent of business leaders say that uncertainty paralyzes them from taking action. Additionally, 34 percent of business leaders responded that the smallest doubt could keep them from acting.[18]

This has been true in spades in digital transformation. According to BT Group research, approximately two-thirds of business leaders say that digital transformation is vital to their company's survival. Yet many are failing to meet expectations because they're suffering from "tech paralysis." BT estimated that 104,000 British businesses would forgo investing in new technology "due to stress associated with the implementation, transformation, and upskilling involved."[19]

Facing the Unknown: Here Be Dragons

In the late Middle Ages, as Europe approached the Age of Sail, mapmakers included elaborate drawings of all manner of strange and menacing creatures in areas of the map that had not yet been explored. The famous phrase "here be dragons" was engraved just below the equator on the Hunt-Lenox Globe, one of the oldest known, dating to about 1510. In addition to gigantic dragons with crimson or emerald-green scales, maps portrayed giant sea lizards with tails the length of three tall ships, dinosaur-sized water pigs, and bizarre amalgams of species, such as the *ichthyocentaur*, which was part human, part horse, and part fish.

Why would mapmakers embellish their wares with such fantastical creatures? While we might think they were gleefully fabricating, historian of cartography Chet Van Duzer explains that "most of the sea monsters reflect an effort on the part of the cartographer to be accurate in the depiction of what lived in the sea."[20] All who might sail into these territories, they warned, faced grave danger. When we're confronting the unknown, our minds can convince us of all sorts of misperceptions and delusions.

The early years of the Age of Sail were, like our current epoch, a period of astonishing change. Navigators were encountering whole new lands. Global trade exploded, bringing new foods and inventions into people's lives, and also new diseases. Port cities boomed, and as one historian describes them, they became places of "opportunity and danger . . . where people of very different origins met for the first time and had to . . . learn from each other."[21] Given all of the new experiences people were exposed to, believing in horrid sea creatures is perhaps quite understandable.

Medieval navigators, traders, and the mapmakers who served them were all wrestling with a huge amount of change and had a hard time coping—and that's what we're struggling with today. The root problem is that we humans generally don't like the level of unknown we're facing in our lives. As a result, many of us are being pushed kicking and screaming into the great unknown, leaving us fearful and exhausted as we're forced to rethink the things we've taken for granted for so long.

Many of us continue to cling to outdated mental maps because they're familiar and comfortable, even if they lead us to constant disappointment because they don't take us to where we want to go. Buddhist monk and scholar Thich Nhat Hanh wrote, "People have a hard time letting go of their suffering. Out of a fear of the unknown, they prefer suffering that is familiar."[22] We must work to change our mindset and learn to embrace uncertainty.

Harvard professor Arthur Brooks, who studies the sources of well-being, has highlighted the following: "Negative emotions help us learn, adapt, and ultimately thrive. As psychotherapist Emmy Gut found in her research, these emotions can be a powerful catalyst for problem-solving, encouraging us to confront issues head-on and find solutions. So, when we feel sadness or anger, it's not just discomfort—it's an opportunity for growth, setting us on a path toward a deeper, more enduring happiness."[23]

Just as negative emotions can guide us to growth and productivity, some fear is justified and can help us take action. The key is to figure out which fears to pay attention to and how to make them constructive. This is something we can only know by getting up close to them.

Optimistic Fear

In 1966, management guru Peter Drucker wrote: "Time is the scarcest resource, and unless it is managed, nothing else can be managed."[24] Today, our scarcest resource is not time but positive energy—the good feelings that help us make the most of our time, build stronger connections, and turn fear into something not only optimistic but productive.

Cornelia calls this *optimistic fear*: a force that harnesses fear as fuel and channels it in constructive ways. Instead of shrinking back, we get closer to the situation, see it more clearly, find more options, and make better decisions. Fear remains a powerful motivator, but optimism transforms it into a spur to productive action. Our eyes stay wide open to the dangers, yet we believe we can rise to the challenge. Optimistic fear also gives us the momentum to engage more deeply with stakeholders—a step that pays off enormously in the long run.

Importantly, optimistic fear isn't about chasing every opportunity. Sometimes the wisest move is to step back, accept a situation, or reduce risk. The difference is that these are deliberate choices rather than reflexive reactions forced on us when we're overwhelmed by what Cornelia has labeled *pessimistic fear*. In that state, anxiety takes over, and we slip into fight, flight, or freeze modes. These reactions may be instinctive, but they do little to help us understand and cope with the continuous change surrounding us.

For example, as employers have introduced AI agents into workplaces, many employees have actively undermined AI initiatives. In one survey, 31 percent of employees questioned responded that they'd consciously tried to sabotage their company's AI strategy. A common reason they gave was fear that their jobs would be displaced.[25] But ironically, they risked losing their jobs if the sabotage were discovered.

Seen from another angle, AI offers abundant opportunities to learn, experiment, and put it to meaningful use. Even high-level leaders can benefit from getting their hands into the details of how AI works. Take the case of Piyush Gupta, the long-serving former CEO and director of Singapore's DBS Group, who led the implementation of AI into the bank's operations. To deepen his own understanding, he even entered Amazon Web Services' DeepRacer League, a competition where participants are exposed to machine-learning training techniques—similar to those that underpin today's most advanced generative AI models—by training autonomous race cars to navigate a simulated track.

Piyush didn't just participate in the race himself—he also encouraged DBS employees to take part. In doing so, he opened the door to being outperformed by his own staff. And they did. As he put it, he "was happy to end up in the top 100 among our people."[26]

Using both curiosity and courage, Piyush engaged his optimistic fear and conquered the unknown. By forging the way in learning, he inspired employees across the bank to embrace AI, helping DBS emerge as a leader in applying artificial intelligence to banking.

The journey from pessimistic fear to optimistic fear starts by opening our minds to the opportunities that come with change. This involves opening our inner lens so that we can see how fear and autopilot might impact how we see the world around us through our outer lens. As we'll explore in the next chapter, this means igniting our curiosity and seeing the unknown as intriguing and full of potential. It also means summoning our courage, facing the challenges ahead, and trusting that exploration will lead us to wiser decisions—and greater strength. When we bring together curiosity and courage—something we call courageous curiosity—we can step into the fast-emerging future with our panoramic intelligence fully engaged, charting our course with optimism, excitement, and a sense of possibility.

Think of those sixteenth-century explorers looking at maps depicting all sorts of ghoulish monsters that awaited their arrival, no doubt licking their chops in anticipation of an easy meal. These sailors had no safe course to follow—and yet they ventured right into those unexplored territories.

In this chapter, we've begun the process of developing our inner lens. We'll continue that work in the next chapter. Before we do, consider the following questions and what they reveal about opportunities to expand your curiosity, operate from a place of optimistic fear, and gather more valuable insights.

QUESTIONS TO CONSIDER

- In what areas of my life do I tend to operate on "human autopilot"? What are the specific benefits I gain from this autopilot mode, and what are the potential risks or missed opportunities?
- As a leader, where might my comfort with "what I already know" be keeping me from seeing emerging risks—or new opportunities—on the horizon?

- How often do I actively seek out contradictory information or dissenting opinions to guard against confirmation bias in my personal decisions?
- How can I convert pessimistic fear to an optimistic one in my approach to uncertainty, and what role might curiosity and courage play in this process?
- What simple acts of courageous curiosity can I take today to explore the "uncharted territory" in my life or work?
- How can I use optimistic fear in a challenging situation to fuel awareness and understanding?

CHAPTER 4

Mindset First

There's a time and a place for replication, for producing the same thing over and over again, with the same look, feel, and quality. One of the things that made McDonald's the global fast-food icon it is today was that if you bought a cheeseburger, fries, and milkshake at a McDonald's restaurant in New York City, you would reliably know the food and packaging you would get if you went back a year later or ordered the same at a McDonald's in Los Angeles or London. As company CEO Ray Kroc explained the secret of his success, "I put the hamburger on the assembly line."[1] That consistency gave customers comfort, which built loyalty.

There's also a time and a place for being creative and innovating, surprising your customers, and maybe even making them just a little bit uncomfortable. This can also build loyalty, maybe even raving fandom. When it comes to food, no one knows this better than Ferran Adrià, the three-star Michelin chef whom "Chef of the Century" Joël Robuchon named "the best on the planet" and *nouvelle cuisine* pioneer Paul Bocuse called "the most exciting."[2] Adrià's restaurant El Bulli, on the Costa Brava in Spain, was crowned the best in the world a record five times by *Restaurant* magazine.

It wasn't through replication that Ferran Adrià reached the pinnacle of success. It was through a completely different mindset.

As an eighteen-year-old with unruly hair and dreams of saving up to fund a trip to Ibiza, Ferran took a job as a dishwasher at a restaurant south of Barcelona. There, he learned to cook basic dishes while memorizing recipes from a classic cooking anthology. After bouncing around different restaurant jobs, Ferran left for his mandatory military service in the Spanish navy, which culminated with him becoming a chef to an admiral.

But Ferran quickly became eager for even more of a challenge, and in 1983, he made the fateful decision to follow his friend Fermí Puig's suggestion to do a one-month stint at El Bulli restaurant. "He told me it was one of the best in Spain, and that it had two Michelin stars," Ferran recalls. "Little did he know that at that time I had no idea what that meant."[3]

Located down a rocky, dusty road that Ferran described as a "veritable goat track," El Bulli overlooked the stunning Platja de Montjoi beach, in a region that was a place of pilgrimage for sun-worshipping tourists. Guests enjoyed an exquisite view of the bay leading to the beach, where the Mediterranean Sea sparkled as though it was covered in diamonds when blessed with the sun's rays.

Ferran enjoyed his "highly intense" month at El Bulli so much that once he completed his military service in 1984, he joined the El Bulli team as a *chef de partie*, beginning what he called a period of "apprenticeship and copying" as he refined his cooking techniques. Within a few months, he'd been promoted to *chef de cuisine* with Christian Lutaud.

However, the very next year, El Bulli suffered a major blow. Michelin demoted the restaurant from two stars to one, and the parade of customers dwindled to the extent that for days and even weeks at a time, the restaurant was only full of empty tables. Yet El Bulli hung on.

Then, in 1987, an unexpected turning point in the restaurant's fortunes arrived. Ferran had recently taken sole charge of the kitchen, and he traveled to Nice on France's Côte d'Azur to attend a demonstration and discussion at the Negresco Hotel featuring the famous chef Jacques Maximin. Ferran recalls:

> One of those attending asked the great French chef what creativity was. Maximin replied: "Creativity means not copying." This simple sentence was what brought about a change in approach in our cooking and was the cutoff point between "re-creation" and a firm decision to become involved in creativity. After getting back to the restaurant, we were convinced that we needed to use major cookery books less and less and try to find an identity of our own. This was the start of our plunge into creativity in El Bulli.[4]

As Ferran told Cornelia, "There's a big difference in procedure between being efficient vs. effective." Copying *nouvelle cuisine* was efficient but not effective in getting more customers. So Ferran "moved from being a technician to a creator."[5]

"Creativity means not copying" became Ferran's personal motto. It was the start of a risky journey in the Michelin world, as he oriented himself away from French cuisine and began charting his own course.

That journey ultimately led Ferran to his greatest innovation. The technique-concept, or "deconstructed cuisine" as he would refer to it, was the "breaking down of familiar dishes into their constituent parts, changing the physical identity of at least some of those parts, and then reassembling the pieces in new ways, so that the dishes take on different forms while retaining sensory connections with their models."[6]

This constant experimentation with new ingredients and cooking techniques led to the creation of such unique El Bulli signatures as frozen chocolate air, gold-tinted caramel of quails' eggs, "vanishing" ravioli, and smoke foam.

It's also a wonderful example of panoramic thinking at its best. As Ferran shared with Cornelia, "You can't be stuck in your own view. You have to have a holistic vision. This is very important. Wine is not a drink. It can be a drink. But someone who cooks with it sees it as an ingredient. Someone who uses it to make vinegar doesn't see it as a drink either. Wine can also be many other things."[7]

This game-changing mindset was integral to El Bulli's team of top chefs. As Ferran put it in conversation with Cornelia:

> Creation at El Bulli was 80 percent individual, 20 percent as a team. Why? Because if we created as a team, everyone would think the same. But if we worked separately, we all thought differently. And this was the magic—our different ways of thinking. Then, there would be a moment when we would bring our ideas together to reflect on them. Each team needs to decide how much they're going to unify and develop separately according to their context, but we need different ideas to come to a better understanding.[8]

The impact of Ferran's application of panoramic thinking in the kitchen was seismic. Ferran's decision to forge a new path, following his curiosity in pursuit of creativity, turned El Bulli around and led it to new heights. As early as 1990, the restaurant celebrated the return of its second Michelin star, confirmation that its new perspective was paying off. By 1997, Ferran's groundbreaking deconstructed cuisine had earned the restaurant its coveted third Michelin star, launching an era in which El Bulli—and its star chef—was showered in accolades and international acclaim.

El Bulli, which seated fifty people, was only open for business from April through September, dinner only. That meant only eight thousand seatings were available each year. The restaurant received more than two million reservation requests annually.

Even though demand for a table at El Bulli was nothing short of extraordinary, Ferran and the team never treated it as their main economic engine, preferring to keep prices deliberately subdued for a restaurant of its caliber. Instead, they developed a constellation of initiatives—from elBullibooks to elBullihotel—which provided the resources to support their true mission: pushing the boundaries of culinary creativity.

For Ferran, these ventures were never an end in themselves but part of a larger journey. Even at the pinnacle of the culinary world, he was excited to plunge further into the unknown and take on new challenges. So in 2011, Ferran Adrià made the momentous decision to close El Bulli, the restaurant that had redefined the very meaning of gastronomy. Behind this decision was a person driven by a relentless desire to explore new horizons and push boundaries. In the restaurant's place, El Bulli 1846, the museum, is now open and carries on the legacy of his creation. Says Ferran about this legacy, "Challenges and curiosity are what drive me. I want to understand more."[9]

Since closing his groundbreaking restaurant, Ferran has addressed over two hundred thousand people, given more than a thousand talks around the globe, and is collaborating on multiple new projects. "I'm happy being driven by my curiosity," he said with a twinkle in his eye.[10] We can't wait to see what's next.

Prepare to Change Your Mindset

Rather than dwelling on the possible downsides of the increased uncertainty and volatility of today's global business environment—looking at it as a glass half empty—we should look at it as a glass half full, or maybe even *completely* full. Uncertainty and volatility bring with them a vast array of opportunities, some we never knew existed before.

To unleash these gifts, we must learn to embrace uncertainty and complexity in a positive way, and that starts with a change of mindset. As we mentioned in the previous chapter, optimistic fear can give us the momentum to get up close to all stakeholders to really understand them. In turn, this helps us evolve our mental map. But doing so requires the right mindset. Growth begins where certainty ends.

The Importance of Curiosity

Natural navigator and author Tristan Gooley has spent decades using his curiosity to decode nature's patterns, uncover hidden insights, and reshape his mental map in ways others might miss. As he shared in his TEDx Talk, "We have to start to notice the things that pass others by." This is just as true for leaders today as it has been for explorers and adventurers of all kinds for millennia. Once we accept this, we begin spotting opportunities others miss. As Tristan explains:

> Things that were once happy to lurk in the background leap forward and begin to fizz in our mind. We notice some wildflowers and they're growing all on their own. And then we think, why are they there? Ah—these wildflowers need more light than the plants around them. How are they getting that light? And it is this that makes us notice that there's a human

> path and there's an intersection with an animal trap. And this opening up of the foliage lets the light in.
>
> And then we think about these beautiful flowers, these balsam flowers. They like damp ground. So, there's probably a river or stream nearby. So, we tune our senses, and we notice the birds in one direction sound different to the birds in another. That's where the river is. And then we remember that these flowers like alkaline soil. We're standing on limestone, and that tells us how the river will behave when the rain from the rainbow hits us. Rivers in limestone country rise very slowly—there are no flash floods. And if we're on limestone, there are probably caves nearby as well.
>
> And then we notice that the plants are aligned. They are all facing the same way to catch the southern light because it is this that attracts their pollinators, the insects. And then we appreciate that these flowers that had been in the background have mapped where the people are, what they're doing, what the animals are doing, where the river is, where the caves are, how the river will behave, and given us a compass.[11]

The Mindset of a Panoramic Leader

Mindsets are remarkably powerful. With the right mindset, you soar higher and see farther as a leader. So it's no surprise that before you embark on the three-step process for becoming a panoramic leader, which is the heart of Part Two, we encourage you to develop what Cornelia has dubbed a *panoramic mindset*.

The good news is that you have the power to change your mindset, as Ferran Adrià did. You can choose to adopt new attitudes anytime you want. Here, we'll describe the ways of thinking that'll allow you to become a panoramic leader.

Adopting a growth mindset is foundational. Stanford University psychology professor Carol Dweck introduced the concepts of *fixed* and *growth* mindsets based on her research with students. Explains Dweck, "In the fixed mindset, students care first and foremost about how they'll be judged: smart or not smart. Repeatedly, students with this mindset reject opportunities to learn if they might make mistakes . . . They are also afraid of effort because effort makes them feel dumb. They believe that if you have the ability, you shouldn't need effort, that ability should bring success all by itself . . . Finally, students in the fixed mindset don't recover well from setbacks."[12]

This mindset can hinder a leader's ability to adapt and grow because it can create resistance to new ideas and defensiveness in the face of feedback. Leaders with a fixed mindset often avoid challenges and may feel threatened by the success of others, which can ultimately stall both their personal growth and the progress of their organization.

A growth mindset is quite the opposite. According to Dweck, in this mindset, "Students care about learning. When they make a mistake or exhibit a deficiency, they correct it. For them, effort is a positive thing: It ignites their intelligence and causes it to grow. In the face of failure, these students escalate their efforts and look for new learning strategies."[13]

Growth-minded leaders tend to be focused on continuous improvement and learning and are more resilient—all important attributes for leaders. They're more likely to embrace change, seek feedback, and involve others in their development process. They believe they can evolve to meet new challenges and, under the right circumstances, accelerate personal growth and organizational effectiveness—especially in times of rapid change and uncertainty.

In your own business, your mindset can have a significant impact on how you lead people. A growth mindset can help you make your team more effective. If you think *they* can't grow their ability and improve—that they just don't have it in them—then, chances are, you won't bother putting much energy into helping them try. But if you think they can always improve, then you'll likely give useful feedback and create opportunities for them. Remember, people can read your belief in them clearly, through your words and your actions.

Having adopted a growth perspective, three additional steps will help enable a panoramic mindset.

Step 1: Ignite Your Courageous Curiosity

Approaching challenges with this mindset opens the door to new ways of thinking and powerful possibilities you might never have imagined. To ignite your courageous curiosity and be inspired, consider the example of young children. They're curious about *everything*. They ask questions fearlessly and aren't self-conscious about what they don't know.

When Cornelia brought her children to the Kennedy Space Center in Florida, they attended a presentation by an astronaut. When her five-year-old son asked him in all sincerity during the question-and-answer session if he'd ever met an alien, after a two-second silence, the whole room—filled with retirees, other children, and working people from a vast range of professions—burst into applause. In that moment, they'd connected with their own sense of deep wonder and were clearly moved by his genuine amazement and desire to learn about what life in outer space might hold in store.

Step 2: Question Yourself

Take a close look at yourself. Do you stick to familiar patterns of behavior, even when they're no longer effective for you? Are you failing to adapt to fast-changing conditions in your industry or in your business? Are you constantly fighting the same fires instead of planning ahead?

If your answer to any of these questions is "yes," don't beat yourself up about that. Here's your opportunity for growth! Make a commitment to rigorously work on changing these behaviors. This is much easier to do if you seek others' viewpoints and listen to them, especially if they contradict your own.

One of Cornelia's clients, Ann, was a newly appointed CEO, taking the reins from the outgoing founder. Although he'd stepped down, the founder continued to pull strings behind the scenes through his relationships with longtime employees. His interference undermined Ann's ability to lead. Who did the company's employees actually report to? Who was really in charge of leading the company? Who was the real CEO?

Ann began to clash with the founder in nearly every conversation and felt increasingly angry and powerless. To help resolve the problem, Cornelia matched her with a peer, Nick, the founder of a different company, for a candid conversation. Like Ann's founder, Nick had faced the emotional challenge of stepping down from a company he'd founded and grown for over a decade. Many of his closest friends were still working there. Stepping down had felt, to him, like leaving a part of himself behind.

During their curated meeting, Ann promised herself to stay genuinely curious about Nick's perspective on the issue. As she listened, she began to understand what it meant to surrender something that had defined your identity for years. What she'd seen as defiance, she now understood as loss.

Nick's story filled Ann with empathy for the founder she'd been so angry with, shifting her perspective. Adding this lesson to her map, Ann decided to reach out to the founder and successfully worked through the issue with him. He agreed to truly let go and trust Ann, and she thrived as CEO, taking the company to the next level of growth.

Step 3: Know Your Map and Keep Adapting It

Ask yourself which parts of your map are no longer accurate. We may think a certain area of our map still holds up well when it really doesn't. Let's say it's your conviction that one of your company's premier products is still superior to that of a competitor who has begun increasing their market share. The product group has been arguing for a major update, but you've held fast to your belief that it's not necessary because sales of this product are still strong—in fact a good deal stronger than those of the competitor. You're sure you're saving loads of money by not launching the upgrade. Nevertheless, you ignite your courageous curiosity and decide to gather some panoramic intelligence.

Speaking with your largest customers, you discover that one of them—a company that's been a reliable bellwether in identifying product trends—thinks you should make the upgrade, and quickly. Grateful for this critical feedback from a key stakeholder, you continue to follow your curiosity and speak with a range of stakeholders to dig into why an upgrade may be advisable or not. You accumulate a treasure trove of data and perspectives. The choice becomes obvious: The upgrade is the best path forward, and you give the product group the green light.

Sometimes when we feel something isn't working, we may be tempted to throw out the entire map and just start over, when, in fact, upon closer examination, it just needs some tweaking. Or we're afraid to admit that one part of it is inaccurate, because we think if we change a part of our map, we risk losing our bearings or invalidating the utility of the whole map. Our inner lens is clouded by fear and uncertainty and it influences our other lenses. But consider this: New lands emerge and geographies change, like volcanic islands literally emerging from the ocean, and they're simply added to existing maps.

Maybe you assume your map is accurate, because things are going smoothly in your career so far. Marshall explains that we get positive reinforcement from our past successes, which can lead us to believe those successes are predictive of great things in the future. He often faces the challenge of helping people realize that sometimes they're successful *in spite of* their behavior and views, not because of them.

If we're overly confident about our map, we'll likely respond badly when someone tells us their perspective doesn't align with it.

Marshall has observed that this often proceeds in three stages.

We think the other person is mistaken. They're relying on incorrect facts and speaking beyond their expertise.

Years ago, Marshall worked with a CEO who was initially dismissive of feedback from his team. He was a brilliant individual with a track record of success. However, his leadership style was perceived as arrogant and unapproachable by his employees. When he received his first feedback report, his immediate reaction was to disregard the negative feedback, thinking that his team was simply confused or wrong.

It dawns on us that maybe the other person is not confused. Maybe, we think, their information about our perceived shortcomings is accurate. But because it can be too hard to deal with the thought that we might be wrong, we're triggered into denial mode. Adam Grant describes the root of the problem in *Think Again*: "When a core belief is questioned . . . we tend to shut down rather than open up. It's as if there's a miniature dictator living inside our heads, controlling the flow of facts to our minds . . . The technical term for this in psychology is the totalitarian ego, and its job is to keep out threatening information."[14]

So we cling to the conviction that our success proves we don't need to change. The criticism couldn't possibly be true. Marshall saw the same behavior in the CEO, who quickly rejected the feedback and avoided what felt unwelcome. His inner lens had closed—and when leaders act untouchable, they become unreachable.

If they keep pressing the issue, we flip to the offense and discredit the person. We think: *Why would a smart person like me listen to a loser like you?* The CEO Marshall was working with reached this stage, trying to guess who'd given the feedback before shooting them down. With support, however, he began to soften his resistance. Following his courageous curiosity, he explored new ways of leading, and in time, his performance steadily improved.

To adapt our map, we need to coach ourselves to let down our defensive guard when people share views or information we disagree with or find threatening. We need to open our inner lens by developing our willingness to change. Ask some questions:

"What happened for them to feel that way?" Really step into their shoes.

"What could be right about what they're saying?" Work to understand why they see things as they do, which will put you in intelligence-gathering mode.

To gain clarity, Patty McCord, former Netflix chief talent officer, suggests asking this simple question: "Can you help me understand what leads you to believe that's true?"[15]

Then we can ask ourselves, "How could I tweak my actions to adapt to that feedback?" We don't need to start from scratch or throw out our entire map. When sailors encounter a problem with their sail, they don't throw out the whole boat. They fix it and continue on. In the 2024–2025 Vendée Globe, a nonstop, solo, round-the-world yacht race nicknamed "The Everest of the Seas," skipper Charlie Dalin had to perform an emergency repair to a damaged sail while in full race mode, working for about thirty-six hours to mend it. He adapted, regained momentum, and eventually won the race in record time, smashing the previous record by a significant margin.

When we encounter new situations or perspectives—whether a torn sail or unexpected feedback—how we respond determines our ability to adapt. By making steady adjustments to our map, we can transform new insights into a deeper understanding that fuels our growth.

How Questioning Yourself Can Help You Make Better Decisions

In their classic book, *Management of Training Programs*, Frank DePhillips, William Berliner, and James Cribbin introduced a four-stage model for learning.

As the authors explain:

> Learning, therefore, is self-development through self-activity. It involves the development of an individual's capacities, the actualization of his potentialities, and the reorganization of his experiences in the direction of what is wiser and better. It is characterized by a passage through four stages: (1) the individual is at first in a state of *unconscious incompetence*, in which he is not even aware of his lack of knowledge; (2) when he becomes aware of his ignorance and the need to do something about it, he enters the stage of *conscious incompetence*; (3) with effort, he succeeds in reaching the third stage, *conscious competence*, in which his knowledge is deliberately and often woodenly

> applied; (4) continued effort may bring him to the level of *unconscious competence*, in which he utilizes his knowledge easily and gracefully as though it was second nature to him.[16]

If we step back for a moment and look at the structure of their model, we can immediately see that very few people would want to be in the first two stages, which represent incompetence. But that's where we usually begin when we start a new job or learn a new task. In the first stage, unconscious incompetence, we don't know what we don't know. When we're true beginners, we don't even understand what we're supposed to do, and we have everything to learn. A danger in this stage for any of us is that because we're oblivious to the knowledge or skills we're missing, we don't understand that we're in this stage. We might develop a false sense of confidence in our abilities, which can lead us to do poor work or make bad decisions without realizing it. That will damage our reputation because others can plainly see our incompetence and that we're blind to it. In this stage, our inner lens is closed, not allowing information gathered by our outer lens to reach our maps.

When we move up to the second stage, we know we're not yet equipped to be successful at a new job or task—we're still incompetent—but at least we're aware of that fact and we understand that we need to learn. A pitfall at this stage is that we may experience increased stress, anxiety, and self-doubt.

As we continue to learn and build our experience, we move up to the third stage, conscious competence. We have the skills and knowledge we need to do the job or task, but we have to think about it—we have to consciously work through at least some of the steps in our mind as we prepare to perform them. In our own reframing of the four-stage model for learning, this is actually a very productive place to be because we're continuously refining our approach to doing our work or solving problems. We're making deliberate choices, noticing what works—and what doesn't—and then adjusting in real time. We're constantly adapting our map with our lenses wide open.

Finally, after we've performed the job or task numerous times, our learning becomes so ingrained within us that we don't have to consciously think about the steps involved to perform them. We've reached the holy grail of learning: unconscious competence, where we can free up our minds to attend to other, higher-level matters by automating tasks unconsciously.[17]

Driving your car is an example, which is why you can have a lively conversation with a passenger as you drive. The same is true for when you walk down the street or ride a bicycle. You don't have to think about *how* to do these things—you just do them.

There are plenty of advantages to reaching the stage of unconscious competence. You're able to perform routine tasks quickly and efficiently while freeing up cognitive resources for other things, which is particularly useful when multitasking or when you're in a complex environment, as so many of us are today. Because tasks require less mental effort when you're unconsciously competent, your cognitive load is reduced, helping to prevent mental fatigue while improving overall performance. You can make decisions more quickly, and you feel more confident and in control.

So you might think that this fourth stage is where you want to be as a leader, and sometimes it is. But being in a state of unconscious competence brings both rewards and significant risks. It's in this stage of competence that we tend to slip into autopilot, putting us in danger of missing signs that we should be adapting to evolving conditions or reaching for new learning—especially in today's world of constant disruption. We become vulnerable to the changing landscape since we're blind to the information we could have gathered if our inner and outer lenses were open.

When we're in unconscious competence, we believe that if we make a mistake, we'll fall into conscious competence, where we're still competent and aware. The problem is, if we're on autopilot, we don't fall from unconscious competence to conscious competence—we can fall catastrophically all the way down to unconscious *in*competence, and we may not even realize it until it's too late.

WHEN MASTERY BECOMES RISK

THE HIDDEN COST OF UNCONSCIOUS COMPETENCE

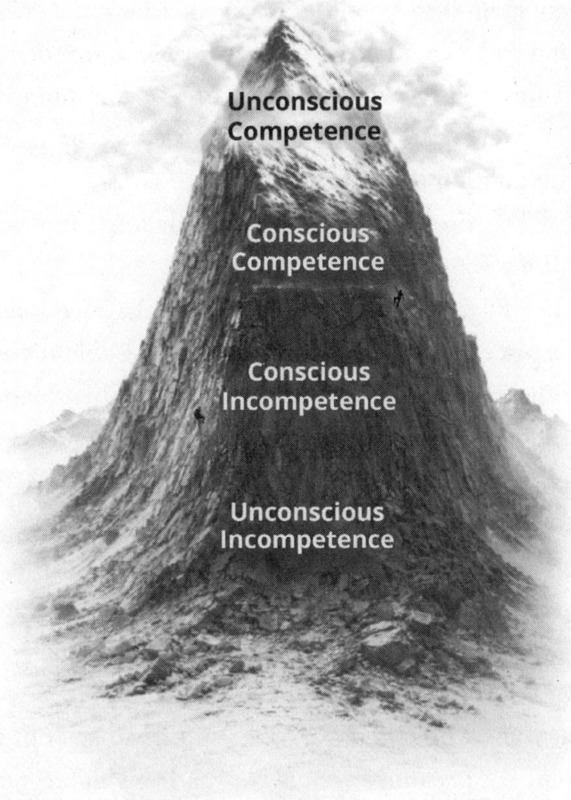

In the popular board game for children in the United States called Chutes and Ladders, the goal is to be the first to move your game piece to the top of the board. Scattered along the route are an array of ladders, which, when you land on them, jump you farther up the board. The chutes, meaning slides, plummet you back down toward the bottom. Leaders who are in the autopilot of unconscious competence aren't in danger of just moving back one or two squares. They're in danger of sliding down a chute all the way to the bottom at any moment. The leader is doing what got them to the top of the organization, or maybe even their industry. Then something happens in the business environment, and what got them there no longer works. But the leader doesn't perceive that and doesn't respond. Expertise can sow the seed of blindness.

Even if we don't slide down a chute, instead continuing to enjoy success, if we stay in the autopilot of unconscious competence, we won't be fulfilling our true potential.

Marshall benefited enormously from being made aware of this at a key juncture of his career.

One of his mentors was Dr. Paul Hersey, a behavioral scientist and influential expert on leadership. He changed Marshall's life in many ways, and one of the transformative lessons he shared was that Marshall was at risk of failing to optimize his potential. One day he said to Marshall, "Your clients love you! The courses you're teaching are incredibly well received. You're getting lots of amazing feedback."

Marshall smiled, thinking Paul was giving him a wonderful pep talk.

Then Paul said, "You are completely screwing up. You are selling the same thing day after day after day. You are not thinking, you are not writing, and you are not developing new material. If you continue doing what you are now, you will have a successful life, but you will never become the person you could be—and you will regret it. You can be more."

That snapped Marshall right out of autopilot. He began to take more time to write new material, and he became focused on his long-term development as a thinker, executive coach, and author, not just on the success he was having as a speaker.

As Marshall reflects back on his life, those four challenging words—*you can be more*—stand out as essential in reigniting his curiosity, leading him on an unceasing quest to learn and grow.

Always keep in mind—add this to your map—that if we want to seize opportunities and manage disruption, we can't settle into the comfort and blindness of unconscious competence. Like Ferran Adrià, we should push ourselves to take on new challenges, always building new knowledge and skills, which require us to continue to open both our inner and outer lenses. Ferran realized that his best pathway was in *conscious* competence, continually questioning himself and even stepping back into conscious incompetence when necessary. By pushing into the uncertain and unfamiliar, he created new dishes and reinvented what a restaurant experience could be.

As psychologist Tasha Eurich wrote in *Insight*, "When it comes to the way we see ourselves, we must be brave enough to spread our wings, but wise enough not to fly too high, lest our blindspots send us soaring straight into the sun. When we learn the truth, it can be surprising, or terrifying, or even gratifying—but no matter what, it gives us the power to improve."[18] In these uncertain and fast-changing times, you don't want to risk being unwittingly thrown down the chute to unconscious incompetence. You want to be constantly open and adaptable, ready to climb the ladder and take on new learning.

Serena's New Map

Imagine you're Serena Williams, widely considered to be one of the greatest tennis players of all time. You're in the first round of the 2012 French Open. Seeded fifth in the tournament, you're looking down the court at Virginie Razzano, the 111th-ranked female tennis player in the world. You've won your opening match in every Grand Slam you've ever played in—forty-six out of forty-six. Today, after three hours and three minutes of a grueling battle, in which you've come within two points of winning the match nine times, including being up five to one in a second set tie-break, Razzano is serving at match point. You are one point from losing.

Razzano's serve is strong. So is your return. She handles it well, rocketing the ball back at you. You strike back with a fierce forehand shot. She fields that too, and you send a crushing backhand missile back over the net . . . just a bit out of bounds.

You've lost.

Tennis fans around the world are shocked, and so are you.

Despite the fact that Serena's performance had been on a slow decline for a while—she hadn't won a Grand Slam tournament in two years—*The New York Times* described her humbling defeat as "an upset that ranked among the most stunning and unexpected in the recent history of the French Open."[19]

We wonder whether Serena thought she might be nearing the end of her remarkable career. She was thirty years old, while the average for women Grand Slam tournament players at the time was just twenty-five. She'd won thirteen Grand Slams. Why wasn't what had gotten her to the top working any longer? Maybe the answer was right there in front of her. Maybe it was time to pass the torch to a younger woman just hitting her peak.

Rather than hang up her racket, though, Serena found a junior tennis academy in Paris where she could spend some time unwinding.

She practiced hitting balls out of view of the press as she digested the events of her devastating defeat. It was there that she met Patrick Mouratoglou, a tennis coach and owner of the academy.

Patrick intently watched Serena as she practiced, closely considering the way she served the ball, how she moved around the court, and the way she volleyed. After forty-five minutes of carefully observing every aspect of Serena's game, he gave her his feedback: "Every time you hit, you're off balance, which makes you miss a lot," he observed. "Also, you lose power because [your] body weight doesn't go through [the shots], and you're not moving up, so your game is slow."[20]

Despite the fact that Patrick had never coached a top-ranked professional player in his life—his experience was limited only to mid-ranked players and below—Serena agreed with the assessment and hit the ground running. What fantastic curiosity. What powerful inner and outer lenses.

Patrick coached Serena for the remainder of the week, showing her insights from his map of how he believed tennis should be played, about balance, momentum, and power. With open lenses, Serena chose to connect new dots and incorporate those learnings into her own map, getting a more multi-dimensional picture of her tennis playing and the game of tennis itself. She then made a pivotal decision: She hired Patrick as her coach. That took great courage. What would the tennis world make of this?

Whatever anyone thought, Serena's panoramic mindset served her extremely well. In the rest of the 2012 season, she defeated Agnieszka Radwańska to win at Wimbledon; she prevailed over Maria Sharapova to earn a gold medal at the Summer Olympics; she beat Victoria Azarenka for the US Open prize; and she closed out the year by toppling Sharapova at the WTA Tour Championships. Serena was a woman transformed.

By the end of her tennis career, she'd won twenty-three Grand Slam tournaments, including the Australian Open (seven times), the French Open (three times), Wimbledon (seven times), and the US Open (six times). In addition, she won seventy-three career singles titles, earning almost $95 million in prize money.

Patrick helped Serena think more panoramically, dramatically widening her perspective as she improved her game. In his book *Unlearn*, business adviser and innovation expert Barry O'Reilly explains, "Patrick helped Serena see the blind spots in her game that she was unaware of, sparking new perspectives, new thinking, and new behaviors. He convinced Serena, for example, of the importance of pre-match preparation, including analyzing each of her opponents, exploring probable game scenarios, and developing tactics to be used during the course of her match."[21]

In describing Serena's transformation, Hall of Fame tennis writer Steve Flink recalled: "Williams was looking at the game very differently, playing with larger imagination, competing with more options, and enjoying herself in the workplace as much as she had in a very long while."[22]

Today, Serena is retired from professional tennis, but she's actively using her panoramic leadership in her own business ventures. These include participating in the ownership group of the WNBA's Toronto Tempo professional basketball team and leading her company, Serena Ventures, which has invested in more than eighty-five companies, at least fourteen of which have reached unicorn status—privately held start-ups worth more than $1 billion.

Serena's journey proves that a truly panoramic mindset can help you redraw the entire landscape of success, one curious, courageous stroke at a time.

In the coming three chapters, we'll introduce you to GEM—a powerful three-step approach for starting your journey to becoming a panoramic leader:

- Step 1: Get up close.
- Step 2: Establish meaningful bonds.
- Step 3: Map your evolving perspective.

QUESTIONS TO CONSIDER

- In what aspects of my life or work am I prioritizing "replication" and consistency, and when might it be more beneficial to embrace creativity and innovation?
- How can I actively cultivate my courageous curiosity to transform uncertainty and volatility into new opportunities?
- How can I open my lenses and genuinely listen to others' viewpoints, especially those that contradict my own, to refine my map?
- Where do I tend to operate with a "fixed mindset," believing my abilities or talents are unchangeable, and how might this be holding me back from personal or professional growth?
- In what areas of my life do I demonstrate a "growth mindset," embracing challenges, learning from mistakes, and persisting despite setbacks?
- What does "I can be more" mean for me in my current stage of life, and what steps can I take to embark on a continuous quest to learn and grow?

PART TWO

THE GEM METHOD: ACTIONABLE STEPS TO PANORAMIC LEADERSHIP

CHAPTER 5

Step 1: Get Up Close

Marshall likes to say that Alan Mulally is one of his three most successful coaching clients (the other two are Frances Hesselbein, former CEO of the Girl Scouts of the USA, and Hubert Joly, former CEO of Best Buy, who you'll meet later in this chapter). Alan is widely considered to be one of the greatest business leaders of our time. He's also one of the best examples of a leader who succeeded by getting up close and engaging with a full array of stakeholders.

After a thirty-seven-year career—culminating in a highly successful eight-year run as president and five years as CEO of Boeing Commercial Airplanes—Alan could have easily called it a day, hanging up his hat and enjoying the retirement he so richly deserved. But instead, he decided to accept one more challenge: joining a whole new industry to turn around the troubled Ford Motor Company as its CEO.

Alan had been brought to Ford in 2006 by none other than Bill Ford, then president, CEO, and board chair. Bill laid out the company's biggest problems. Ford was losing so much money that some analysts questioned whether it could survive. Recalls Alan, "The forecast for profits for 2006, for automotive, was for a $17 billion loss. And at the end of the year, we achieved that loss."[1]

To turn the company around, Alan would have to sell off underperforming brands, close factories, lay off workers, find efficiencies wherever he could, bring together his global team, and keep the workers' unions and the global dealer network happy—all while building cars that would entice customers to open up their wallets. A tall order, and to many in the industry, a seemingly impossible one.

Alan knew just how vital it would be to sit down with stakeholders across the board. Conversations with this wide spectrum of people would help him recognize critical issues that otherwise rarely surface in strategic planning. From his years at Boeing, he'd learned that success requires more than a brilliant plan. As he said in an interview, "Everybody needs to be included—all the consumers, the traveling public, our employees, the suppliers, the financiers, the regulatory agencies."[2]

He met with employees from all around the company. Outside the company, he met with suppliers, dealership owners, investors, bankers, government regulators, union leaders, and even with leading competitor GM's CEO, Rick Wagoner. To capture their input, Alan wrote detailed summaries after each meeting and kept them in binders in his office.

In his second year, he even spent a day working at two dealerships to better understand the experiences of salespeople and customers. At one, a woman arrived with her two sons, explaining she was choosing between a Toyota Camry and a Ford Fusion. Alan described the Fusion's features and chatted with her sons while she explored the car. One boy lifted his shirt and asked Alan, "Do you want to see my surgical scars?" He had staples across his chest. Alan was deeply moved that despite what was clearly a major surgery, he felt it was important to accompany his mother and help her make this decision. Alan recalls how this reinforced for him the importance of Ford's responsibility to those who buy their cars.[3]

The links Alan forged with stakeholders, one by one, person by person, became an incredibly strong chain. It's no accident that during Alan's tenure at Ford, employee satisfaction skyrocketed and Alan's approval rating reached 97 percent.[4]

One story he tells of stakeholder interactions in those days especially stands out.

Together with a large number of the company's employees, four thousand Ford dealership owners assembled at Ford Field—the stadium where the Detroit Lions football team plays. Now, it's important to understand that the dealers had generally not been pleased with Ford's management; they felt their concerns had not been listened to. So, this could have been seen as a journey into the belly of the beast for the CEO. Instead, Alan approached it as an opportunity to make a dramatic demonstration of appreciation for the dealers.

After telling the gathered dealers that the company planned to offer them a fuller range of vehicles, and after sharing more of his turnaround strategy, he told them that they would be an important part of the plan, "because no one in Detroit sells any cars or trucks, and you have the best relationships with your customers and your clients. So, we're going to work really closely with you."

Alan then asked all of the Ford employees present, who were seated at the front of the crowd, to stand up and turn around to face the dealers seated behind them. He said to the employees, "I want you to tell the dealers that you love them." He heard a low murmur of mumbled words, "We love you." Not satisfied with the performance, he told them to say it again like they meant it, and the employees belted out "We love you!" in a ringing chorus. The dealers responded by breaking out in applause.[5]

As Dave Wilson, a dealer and recipient of this promise made by Ford executives, shares of Alan, "He truly inspired everyone that could be inspired at Ford Field that day. I believed that this was the man who would give it his all to right the ship and take Ford to levels no one could ever imagine."[6]

Alan stayed true to the promise to involve the dealers in the turnaround, and he credits them with important inputs in ensuring Ford produced the cars customers wanted.

This commitment to empathy was not softness; it was strength. Alan's leadership demonstrated that deep care for people and uncompromising performance can—and must—coexist. As New Zealand's former Prime Minister Jacinda Ardern once observed, "You can be kind but strong, empathetic but decisive, optimistic but focused."[7] Alan embodied that balance. By leading through both heart and discipline, Alan modeled a form of panoramic leadership that united insight with action.

Remove Your Obstacles to Getting Up Close

It's easy for us to tell you that you need to get up close to the people, situations, or problems that you want to understand better. We appreciate that actually doing so can seem difficult, even uncomfortable. For one thing, we're all so busy just trying to attend to the tasks and problems right in front of us. How can we make time to go gallivanting around to far corners of our company, let alone seek out customers, suppliers, or retailers? Not to mention people in the community who aren't even involved in the business.

More than just time, getting up close requires opening all three of our lenses. A wider inner lens helps us stay open-minded so that we're more willing to get up close to stakeholders. A wider outer lens helps us engage with stakeholders more panoramically. And our relational lens helps us integrate what we learn, updating our maps so we can lead with greater clarity and connection.

When it comes to using our outer lens, getting up close to our stakeholders doesn't have to take much time. You can make it an efficient process, finding ways to work some outreach into your regular routines, which may involve staying in touch with a given stakeholder once a month or even a few times a year. Interacting with stakeholders can become part of your regular schedule.

Another CEO who was a big practitioner of getting up close is former head of PepsiCo, Indra Nooyi. She recounts in her memoir that she found going out to stores so valuable that she would get "out in the marketplace almost every week." One time, she decided to sit in her car for a while with Brian Cornell, head of PepsiCo America Foods, and just watch shoppers entering and exiting a Publix grocery store. Indra was struck by how many of the older people would stop and chat for a bit after leaving the store. She realized that "shopping was clearly a happy occasion for them."[8]

When the two executives went inside the store for a usual spin around, with those older shoppers on her mind, Indra had an "aha" moment. All of the Pepsi soda and bottled water in the store was in twenty-four-pack cases. Such large cases must be a horribly heavy lift for those older people, she realized. That led her to send a team of PepsiCo employees to the MIT AgeLab to learn how to tailor features of PepsiCo products for the elderly, such as labeling, typefaces, and ergonomics.

On a more uncomfortable note, Indra was approached by activist investor Nelson Peltz, whose white paper had proposed breaking PepsiCo in two, dividing the snacks and drinks businesses. Many CEOs would have allowed the fear of the unknown or complacency to lead them to either confront or dismiss Nelson, especially as he was proposing such an aggressive change.

Instead, Indra got up close and met with Nelson, treating him with respect and assuring him that she would take his paper seriously.

In fact, Indra did discuss his proposal in great detail with the board, but in the end she saw that the company was stronger combined than separate. She decided not to follow through with his proposal, while still meeting with Nelson whenever he asked for time. When Nelson did sell his PepsiCo shares, it was at more than a 30 percent profit.[9]

Getting up close to some stakeholders might seem like a daunting task. And yet, as Brené Brown writes in *Daring Greatly*, "Connection is why we're here; it's what gives purpose and meaning to our lives." True connection, whether between a leader and their team or between peers across borders, is built through presence, vulnerability, and genuine care.[10] It's what transforms shared purpose into shared momentum.

Still, hesitation is natural. How will we strike up a conversation with them? Will they want to hear from us? Will they think it's strange that we're reaching out to them? Some fascinating research by professors Nicholas Epley and Juliana Schroeder will hopefully inspire you to go ahead and get past that discomfort. They stated, "For a species that seems to benefit so much from connecting to others, why would people in close proximity so routinely seem to prefer isolation instead? Why are such highly social animals, at times, so distinctly unsocial?"[11]

To investigate, they conducted a series of experiments, including with Chicago-area commuters, to examine how people interact with strangers. To kick things off, participants were assigned one of three different scenarios for their commute: "Connect with a stranger near them, to remain disconnected, or to commute as normal." They were then asked to fill out a survey designed to measure the consequences of connection versus solitude.

Now, as we're sure you can appreciate, approaching a total stranger and engaging them in conversation can be horribly uncomfortable. So the survey results were striking. The participants who connected with strangers "reported having the most positive experience out of all three of our experimental conditions. Most importantly, participants in the connection condition reported having a significantly more positive experience than participants in the solitude condition."[12] In other words, the people who struck up conversations with strangers during their commute reported feeling happier than those who did not.

Conversation is energizing. And when we encounter someone and chat with them, it uplifts us. We're excited to be seen by someone—it makes us feel like we belong, that we're connected. And yet, we often avoid talking with strangers. Can you remember the last time you struck up a conversation with a stranger in an elevator, on a public bus, or on a subway?

We can understand if you think, *Okay, maybe talking with strangers can be a pleasant surprise*, but what about talking with disgruntled stakeholders? Is it worth the discomfort? Yes, because they're likely to offer you some of the most valuable insights of all.

Consider unhappy customers. The business breakthroughs that have resulted from developing an understanding of their irritations are legion. We'll recount just one.

Airbnb struggled to gain traction early on, threatening the company's viability. The founders got close to the problem. They met with Paul Graham, founder of the start-up accelerator Y Combinator, which advises entrepreneurs in its program, and they scoured the Airbnb website with him. Through this process, they discovered that for many properties that weren't performing well, the photos were making a bad impression with prospective customers, stunting company growth. Says cofounder Joe Gebbia, "The photos were not great photos. People were using their camera phones or using their images from classified sites. It actually wasn't a surprise that people weren't booking rooms because you couldn't even really see what it is that you were paying for."[13]

Graham suggested that the founders visit a number of properties in

New York City that were performing poorly, bring a high-quality camera, and meet with the hosts to discuss the problem and take better photos. Within a week, rentals of the properties increased substantially. So the founders launched the Airbnb photography program, which allowed hosts to schedule professional photographers to take photos of their property on the company's dime. As a direct result, Airbnb bookings climbed significantly, putting the company on the path to success.

Over time, the founders developed an appreciation for understanding the desires, worries, and challenges of their hosts and guests, such as hosts' concerns that they were allowing strangers into their homes, and they communicated the importance of this level of empathy to all of their employees. One way they did this was by hiring a top-rate storyboarder who had worked with Pixar.

Storyboards are vignettes depicting part of the story of a film. In this case, the storyboards depicted parts of the host and guest experiences, such as showing a host couple together at their computer and excited by seeing that they'd just gotten a booking, and for guests, arriving at the rental and being delighted by it. The storyboards were posted on the walls of the office to remind employees of the importance of getting up close to all the people they were serving.

Who's Not at Your Table?

As you get up close, you might wonder exactly who you should get closer to. Our answer is simple: You get up close to people who are near you, people who are far from you, and people who are everywhere in between. Your outer lens will be most powerful when you're including the full panorama, both inside the company and outside of the company. It's crucial to talk to people not in your day-to-day circle.

Which leads us to this question: Who's not at your table?

We often fall into autopilot and invite the same people to our table that we always do. That may be our leadership team, a trusted colleague, a business partner, close friends, or our spouse. It's natural for us to form these kinds of exclusively close relationships with those we know and trust and to lean particularly heavily on them for their inputs and opinions. However, by getting up close to people whom we don't traditionally invite to join us at the table, we'll learn new things, gain new perspectives, and grow our relationships with them. And in the process, we may discover partners we didn't realize we had, just as Alan Mulally partnered with dealers, many of whom had been disgruntled but became fonts of valuable input and key partners for Ford.

As we seek out stakeholders, we should specifically reach out to people who are different from us in experiences, concerns, and interests. As Harvard professor Arthur Brooks explains, "Compatibility keeps us connected, but it's our differences that drive us forward. True growth in relationships comes not just from what aligns, but from what complements."[14]

You may also want to get up close with people you aren't likely to actually meet, such as the leaders, musical artists, actors, and athletes whom you admire or even fictional characters who are central to a book or film that you love. Bonds of this kind are called *parasocial* relationships. Says Arthur Brooks, "Humans have evolved to thrive in groups, probably because prehistorically, you needed to rely on other people to survive by building social relationships. And so we become attracted to and care about people if we have a regular enough exposure to them."[15] This is the case, whether or not we know them personally.

Reading about people, watching interviews, and listening to podcasts offer valuable windows into the thoughts and experiences of those who think differently from us. They can also inspire us to connect with them, as we discover shared values and interests through their stories.

Learning about others' lives can also teach us a great deal about the world and about the importance of looking at it from different perspectives. In the documentary *Jane*, directed by Brett Morgen, we're given a rare, intimate window into the life of Jane Goodall, PhD, DBE. She was the founder of the Jane Goodall Institute, a UN Messenger of Peace, and the world's foremost expert on chimpanzees. The film carries us into the forests of Gombe in western Tanzania, where we learn about Jane's remarkable curiosity and patience.

Beyond the documentary, let's step into Jane's story. She grew up in England, the daughter of a businessman father and a novelist mother. Early in life, she developed a love for books, exploring those in her own home but also spending hours at a local secondhand book shop. Her family didn't have money for her to buy books, so she would save up any money she earned or received as a gift to spend at the shop.[16] She was especially drawn to stories of far-off lands and animals. Two of her favorites, *Tarzan* and *Doctor Dolittle*, fed her imagination and created a dream to one day go to Africa to see the animals she'd only read about.

At twenty-three, after working as a secretary to save money for that dream, Jane accepted an invitation to visit a school friend at her family farm in Kenya. Once there, she met Dr. Louis Leakey, a paleoanthropologist and archaeologist who, along with his wife Mary, would later that year make groundbreaking discoveries proving that humans originated in Africa.

At the time, he'd just lost his secretary, and since Jane had secretarial skills, she immediately applied for the job. Dr. Leakey was impressed with Jane's knowledge of animals and invited her to accompany him and his wife, Mary, on a research trip to Olduvai Gorge. One evening, around the campfire, Jane recounted how she'd calmly handled an encounter with a young lion—an experience she believed helped convince Dr. Leakey she was the right person to go study chimpanzees.

As it turned out, it was Jane's mixture of patience, keen observation, and extensive knowledge of animals that led Dr. Leakey to see her as uniquely prepared to study the chimpanzee community in Tanzania and "observe things that those in the existing scientific community would not be able to."[17] Jane had neither formal scientific training nor a university degree—something that could challenge the credibility of her research, especially in light of the groundbreaking level of discoveries Leakey hoped she would make.

At the time, scientists believed that some behaviors were uniquely human—especially the ability to make and use tools (humans were then defined as "man, the toolmaker"). Leakey wanted to investigate whether those beliefs were truly the case.

In fact, he "felt that Jane's lack of formal academic training was advantageous because she would not be biased by traditional thought and could study chimpanzees with an open mind"[18] and that "a mind uncluttered by academia would yield a fresh perspective."[19] Inspired by these beliefs, in 1960, Leakey sent Jane to Gombe, on the eastern shores of Lake Tanganyika in Tanzania, to do just that.

However, local authorities insisted that it was impossible for a young woman to travel there alone. So Jane's mother, Vanne, agreed to accompany her. Dr. Leakey had warned her that the journey to Gombe could be a dangerous one. There had been a revolt in the nearby Belgian Congo, and the region was in turmoil. The air was oppressive, the humidity unbearable, and the downpours unceasing. Added to that, Jane developed a malaria-like fever when she first arrived. Could she withstand the elements and the diseases she encountered?

And who was she to be researching chimpanzees? She was "just a secretary," after all, without formal training for such a job. Would anyone give her conclusions any credence?

Finally, there was the fear that came from knowing that she only had six months' funding for her expedition—if funds ran out, would she be forced to abandon her quest?

Jane spent months trying to get up close to the Gombe chimpanzees. The hillsides were steep and the distances vast, and whenever she did spot chimps, they would immediately run away in fear. As time passed, this led to much disappointment and uncertainty. Would she ever gain their trust?

One day, a few months into her stay, an older chimpanzee—whom she named David Greybeard—allowed her to observe him. His acceptance of her presence allowed other chimpanzees in the Gombe community to follow suit. Jane started to observe their behavior in great detail.

Her patience and keen powers of observation soon yielded astonishing results. A few months after arriving, she made a discovery that would shock the world: Chimpanzees not only used tools—they made them. A few years later, these observations would overturn long-held scientific beliefs and forever reshape the way we humans understand our place in the natural world.

Dr. Leakey realized Jane's work would carry far greater weight if she obtained a degree, so he arranged for her to pursue a PhD in Ethology at Newnham College, University of Cambridge, even though she had no basic bachelor's degree. In 1966, she earned her PhD and continued her research in what is today Gombe National Park. The study she began in Tanzania in 1960, at just twenty-six years old, continues to this day.

Jane's groundbreaking discoveries emerged from a rare convergence: her patience, persistence, and the stories that first drew her to Kenya—together with Dr. Leakey's uncommon foresight to see great potential in Jane.

Her story reminds us that innovation often begins with unlikely voices that the world overlooks. As you build your panoramic intelligence, ask yourself, "Who's at my table?" If the people assembled there are too much like you—they think like you, they act like you, they have the same experiences as you, they nod their heads in agreement with everything you say, they don't bring anything new and fresh and maybe even controversial to the table—then make a point of interacting with others who do. And learn from their perspectives.

Strategically Selected Differences

Earlier, we introduced you to the Leaders' Circles that are at the heart of Cornelia's peer coaching process. These small, moderated groups bring senior leaders into a safe, confidential space where they can test bold ideas, tackle tough challenges, and support one another. Cornelia purposefully curates each circle, bringing together people whose differences are strategic and complementary, while ensuring they also share common experiences that connect them with the other senior leaders in the group.

Because leaders rarely have access to a space where they can truly open up, be vulnerable, and tap into their peers' expertise, the time spent in these circles is invaluable. Let's take a closer look at how the circles help them get up close to their most difficult problems and uncover more solutions.

Cornelia starts by asking each leader to share their life story, specifically leading with what's *not* on their résumé. This allows the peers to see one another's passions and goals and the journey that shaped their outlook. They share stories about the questions they faced in childhood—and the ones they face now—the challenges they've overcome, and the lessons they keep close to their hearts.

These moments have a quiet power. As the stories unfold, Cornelia sees an expression soften when a participant hears about a family situation that mirrors their own. Eyes brighten when a member describes a cherished place in the world. Trust builds as peers realize that others have faced similar trials and understand what they've been through.

From there, the leaders take turns presenting the issues they want to discuss. They use their combined experience to pose questions that explore and redefine these issues, since thoughtful questions often lead to answers more effectively than direct suggestions.

One participant in Cornelia's circle, Robert, had been the CEO of a global company for seven years and was stepping down. A native of the European country where the company was headquartered, he'd spent more than two decades helping it grow from a regional enterprise into an international leader. His successor, an American, had recently been announced.

Robert supported this appointment, but saw tension building. A few leaders still resisted the idea of a non-European CEO, and the threat of a rift dividing the senior management team was real. He'd worked with the board on a smooth handover and had already started preparing the ground for the transition, bringing his European and North American teams together at an off-site. However, this was clearly not enough.

With only a short window before the incoming CEO assumed his new role, Robert took this problem to his circle of peers.

"Robert, do you think you might have already decided who's worth supporting, and who isn't, in this conflict?" inquired Brian, another CEO. "From my own experience, when I first stepped into a similar role, a few of the long-serving leaders stacked the deck against me and questioned my authority. We only made progress when I stopped and took their concerns seriously. I wasn't aware that I'd already written these leaders off in my mind."

Considering Brian's question, Robert had an "aha" moment. He realized that although he was still working with these disgruntled leaders, he'd begun to dismiss them in his mind. But if he wanted his successor to start on a level playing field, he needed to resolve this underlying tension—even if he saw these leaders as stubborn or defensive—by treating their pushback as legitimate and worthy of being taken seriously. Letting go of his judgments would be harder than implementing any structural change. But he resolved to do it—and to get up close to the tension instead of managing it from a distance. *Less labeling, more listening,* he told himself.

Over the following weeks, Robert initiated direct, candid conversations—listening carefully, addressing specific concerns, and clarifying expectations. Gradually, he reached an understanding with each of them. One left by mutual agreement and the other committed to giving the incoming CEO a fair chance.

When the successor formally assumed his role, the leadership team welcomed the new CEO without any major issues, and Robert remained visibly supportive through the handover phase. The company avoided a leadership crisis and turned a potential fracture into the foundation for its next era of international growth.

Getting Up Close to New Ideas

Although much of the focus of this chapter has been on getting up close to other people, it's important to remember that we can (and should) also get up close to *ideas*, especially new ones. Jack Sim, who grew up in the slums of Singapore, lifted himself out of poverty to become an accomplished entrepreneur, founding a series of sixteen successful companies. These companies included a clay roof tile factory, which he cofounded in Malaysia, called Besco Building Supplies. When the Asian currency crisis hit in 1997, Besco's business drastically declined, and Jack's partners, including Saint-Gobain, a French multinational corporation, decided to sell their stakes in the company. Selling those shares to other investors looked unlikely, and Besco's future hung in the balance.

Jack and his brother William, who owned 10 percent and 5 percent of the company, respectively, decided to buy the remaining 85 percent of the shares that their partners were offering and turn the company around. Jack mortgaged his house, and his wife emptied her life savings to pay their partners out in cash.

Leading the turnaround was traumatic for Jack. He feared employees would abandon the company. As he drove to work, he imagined their resignation letters piling up on his desk. He recalled to Cornelia, "I felt like a failure because I couldn't retain employees who'd worked with me for so long that they became friends."[20]

To maintain his mental and emotional health while he turned Besco around to profitability, Jack got up close to a new idea and made an audacious decision that bucked traditional chief executive norms: He would work only half of each day at the company and dedicate the other half to founding a social enterprise. This seemingly counterintuitive move—especially in the face of Besco's very real challenges—would open his mind to even more new ideas and possibilities, which he believed would ultimately benefit the business.

The organization he launched was the World Toilet Organization (WTO), a global nonprofit organization committed to improving sanitation conditions around the world.[21] According to a World Health Organization report, 1.5 billion people worldwide lack basic sanitation services,[22] and more than half a million people die each year due to unsafe sanitation.[23]

"People around me thought I was crazy," he told Cornelia. "They asked how I could volunteer my time when my business needed me so much." What they didn't know was that his work on the WTO helped him manage his stress and provided him with the mental strength he needed for the turnaround. Jack explained that "giving service" and the WTO work energized him. By devoting himself to a larger social good, he restored his sense of self-worth. "Crisis management means managing the business, but also managing yourself," he shared. "If you don't manage yourself, you can't manage the business. When you have self-worth, then you can manage everything around you."[24]

He recalled that during the turnaround crisis, an employee had said to him, "I'm really so sad for you because I can resign, but bosses can't resign." Once again bucking traditional chief executive norms, he asked himself this question: Why *can't* I resign once the turnaround is complete?

And as it turned out, Jack realized he could.

After Besco became securely profitable, he transitioned the company's operations to other leaders, trusting them to run the business, and he focused more on volunteer work. Today, Jack continues to devote large amounts of his time to social causes, including spearheading sanitation initiatives, contributing to food-relief efforts, and founding the Bottom of the Pyramid Hub, which works to find business solutions for alleviating poverty.

In these endeavors, Jack demonstrates panoramic leadership by getting up close to problems, the people affected by them, and those who can help him reach his goals. In one instance, he wondered why people in some remote areas of China didn't have flush toilets. Curious, he decided to visit and find out for himself. What he discovered surprised him. Many people who lived in these areas were quite well off. They lived in big houses, and they owned cars, televisions, washing machines, water heaters, and other modern conveniences. Surely, he assumed, flush toilets would be part of that picture.

They weren't. Jack couldn't find a single one. Not even in the wealthiest homes. Flush toilets simply weren't part of daily life. The barrier wasn't money. It was mindset and habit. He updated his map: Wealth alone doesn't drive change. Culture, habits, and awareness are just as important.

Jack attests to the enormous value of gathering panoramic intelligence: "I try to have 360 degrees of exposure. I go to poor villages and slums and examine the conditions there, and then at other times work with the United Nations, the Clinton Global Initiative, the World Economic Forum, and the Gates Foundation. I've worked with prime ministers and presidents, and I also became a professor at the Lee Kuan Yew School of Public Policy at the National University of Singapore. All of these relationships and experiences are important for me in learning what I need for my job, and I'm very grateful to share this journey with so many others."[25]

Traversing Foreign Terrain

Engaging with stakeholders is crucial when expanding into new business areas. Their insights can spark breakthroughs that lead to game-changing partnerships. Consider the case of Hubert Joly.

Hubert became president and CEO of Best Buy in August 2012, and he led the company until he stepped down as executive chairman in June 2020. Marshall first became Hubert's coach in his previous position as CEO of the Carlson Companies, the Minneapolis-based hospitality giant, and this relationship continued when Hubert moved to Best Buy. He's widely credited with turning the company around—saving it from near collapse and steering it onto a path of remarkable growth.

Battered by the unrelenting assault of low-cost online retailers, especially Amazon, Best Buy appeared ready to follow in the not-so-jolly shoes of Circuit City, once a dominant force in consumer electronics retailing but declining for years before it shut down in 2009. On top of that, some of Best Buy's key vendors, including Apple, Microsoft, and Sony, were building their own stores, opening a troubling new front in the retail wars.

Hubert recalls that when he was considering leaving his position at Carlson to take the Best Buy job, "Some of my friends thought . . . I was either crazy or suicidal. This was the all-you-can-eat menu of challenges. Everybody thought we were going to die."[26]

In addition to the problems in the business, a struggle for control of the company was underway. The company founder and former chairman and CEO, Dick Schulze, had launched an effort to raise the funds to buy the company and take it private. If he succeeded, where would that leave Hubert? Schulze and his partners might well want to replace him with their own choice. On top of all this, Hubert reflects, "I knew nothing about retail."[27] He had never worked for a retail company.

But Hubert was intrigued by the prospect. He was familiar with Best Buy's business to some extent from living in Minneapolis, where the company is headquartered. He'd also spearheaded the appointment of longtime Best Buy CEO Brad Anderson to the Carlson board because he was impressed by Anderson's work in building the company with Schulze. Yet Hubert realized he should now learn all he could about the company, not only by reading voluminous material but also by getting up close.

He started by going to a Best Buy store in Edina, a town near Minneapolis, where he immediately began to perceive why the company was struggling. He described the store as "an uninspiring, dark, deserted cave."[28] No salesperson came to see if they could help him as he walked around; a group of them were hanging out together, chatting.

Hubert had decided that in addition to touring the store, he would become a customer, and he picked out a phone screen protector and asked the group of sales associates if someone could help him put the protector on his phone. One of them responded that he would do so and the charge would be $18. That was a stunning indication that the company wasn't emphasizing customer service.

After Hubert visited another store, this time buying a new phone, for which he had to sign up to the service offering it, he found himself in what he described as a "Kafkian world" of customer support, actually unable to get a support technician to speak with him. These frustrations spurred him on to conduct a raft of reconnaissance. All the legwork convinced him to take the job because it revealed to him that, as challenging as the competitive environment was, the company's "problems were largely self-inflicted."[29] That meant that he could find ways to fix them. But not on his own.

Hubert didn't stop getting up close after he stepped into the CEO role. For his first few days on the job, he actually worked in a Best Buy store, wearing the distinctive sales associate outfit of blue shirt and khakis, and a tag saying, "CEO in Training." He thoughtfully observed the action, interacted with employees and customers, and spent quality time getting to know some of the staff after work hours, away from "the office." He recalls,

> After my shift, I had dinner with the store management team at a local pizzeria. We spent the evening chatting and getting to know each other while also discussing what was working well for them and what was not. These were people coming face to face with customers every day, having to do their job with whatever tools had been given to them. They knew a lot about what was really going on at Best Buy. A lot![30]

By getting up close and embracing this crucial step of panoramic leadership, that dinner helped Hubert gain a much wider perspective of the depth of Best Buy's problems. In one example, a sales associate showed Hubert what happened when you searched the Best Buy website for a common item. When she typed "Cinderella" into the search bar, the result was a list of Nikon cameras. In another example, Hubert was told that the employees were unhappy because their employee discounts had been reduced. He explains, "Part of the reason many Blue Shirts worked at Best Buy was because they loved electronics, and the decision to push back a perk that they dearly valued bit hard."[31]

By getting up close to his stakeholders, everyone from employees to vendor CEOs and suppliers, Hubert was able to build threads of connection with them that he could weave into strong ropes to explore new areas of business and pull the company up the mountain of success.

In the next chapter, we explore how to build connections that enable panoramic leadership. But before we turn to that, here are some questions to help you get up close to your stakeholders, problems, and opportunities.

QUESTIONS TO CONSIDER

- How can I get up close to different stakeholders? Can I reach out and speak with them? Can I read about them?
- How can I get up close to new ideas? Where can I find them?
- When I've engaged with someone or something unfamiliar, what surprising insights or positive experiences resulted from that connection?

- Which fears did I have to overcome to form the relationships that are now central to my life?
- Which stakeholders are not at my table and how can I invite them to join?
- Whose perspectives—distinctly different from my own—have most deeply expanded my understanding or challenged my personal map?

CHAPTER 6

Step 2: Establish Meaningful Bonds

During the fourth century BCE, the known world of European mapmakers was largely contained within the borders of the Persian Empire, parts of Mesopotamia, and the Mediterranean basin. For the people who inhabited these areas, the rest of the world was a mystery, though some made conjectures about it. The Greek philosopher Aristotle came up with the idea that there must be a very large, unknown landmass south of the equator because that would be a counterbalance to the known lands north of the equator. This was based on his belief that the natural world was ruled by symmetry.[1]

Over time, this hypothetical land became known as *Terra Australis Incognita*, or "unknown land of the south," and it loomed large in the imaginations—and the dreams—of kings and queens, empire builders, explorers, adventurers, and fortune seekers who hoped to discover and claim it for their own, tapping immense riches that legend said were waiting there. And because of all this dreaming, numerous expeditions were launched.

In 1755, at the age of twenty-six, with eight years of civilian mercantile sailing experience already under his belt, James Cook made the bold decision to resign from his secure position with the English merchant service to enlist in the British Royal Navy. While there's been much speculation as to why he took this big step into the unknown—where he might be ordered to sail to exotic but potentially dangerous places like the West and East Indies—according to an article published by the Captain Cook Society, "From the little we know of Cook's personality, he continually strove to extend himself and to experience new things."[2]

Cook quickly rose up through the ranks and proved himself an exceptionally talented navigator and mapmaker. In 1768, he was promoted to lieutenant and put in command of the Royal Navy ship *Endeavour* on a mission commissioned by the Royal Society to sail to Tahiti and witness the transit of Venus. There, scientists in the crew would establish an observatory to study the passage of this planet between the Sun and the Earth, part of a phenomenon that repeats only once every 243 years. Measurements taken during the transit would help British astronomers calculate the distance between the Sun and the Earth—the *astronomical unit*, considered at the time to be the cosmic Holy Grail.

To Cook's good fortune, he was also tasked with bringing along botanist Joseph Banks, whose job it was to record his observations of the people, flora, and fauna they encountered during their voyage and to collect natural history specimens and bring them back to England.[3]

Yet another order given to Cook was kept secret from him, in a missive he was to open only after he'd made the observations of the transit of Venus. Cook's team successfully established the observatory on Tahiti, and right on schedule, on June 3, 1769, they watched Venus make its transit. Time to open the secret instruction: "Proceed to the southward in order to make discovery of the Continent . . . until you arrive in the Latitude of 40°, unless you sooner fall in with it. But not having discover'd it or any Evident signs of it in that Run, you are to proceed in search of it to the Westward."[4]

The continent referred to in these secret orders was the fabled land of *Terra Australis Incognita*.

Before the *Endeavour* sailed south, Joseph Banks suggested Cook invite a man he'd met to join the expedition. Named Tupaia, he was from Raiatea in the Society Islands northwest of Tahiti. Of noble birth, strong, handsome, and athletic, Tupaia was a priest trained in traditional navigation with remarkable skill in mapmaking. Banks knew that Tupaia's extensive knowledge of the islands of French Polynesia and beyond and ways to navigate through them would be of immeasurable value to Cook. Tupaia also knew which islands were inhabited and the names of some chiefs—and he might be helpful in communicating with them.

The *Endeavour* departed from Tahiti on July 13, 1769, and once it reached 40° south, with *Terra Australis Incognita* nowhere in sight (the continent, later given the name Antarctica, remained undiscovered for another fifty years), Cook turned his ship to the west. Almost three months after they left Tahiti—in October 1769—a cabin boy spotted land, and two days after that they made landfall in Poverty Bay on the east coast of New Zealand's North Island—a first-time visit to New Zealand for both Tupaia and Cook. They eventually circumnavigated and mapped the entirety of New Zealand together.

As they explored these lands, Tupaia contributed to Cook's mission over and over again, acting as an interpreter and an ambassador. He not only smoothed relations with the Māori people who lived in New Zealand, but they also treated him as an honored guest, enfolding him in valuable cloaks and entrusting him with ancient treasures.

Tupaia and Cook were unlikely associates in exploration, but they established a panoramic partnership, enabling them to explore lands that neither had previously ventured into on his own. Their success relied on trust and mutual understanding—qualities essential for building strong relationships with stakeholders.

Connecting with Stakeholders

The next step in developing panoramic leadership is to go beyond understanding stakeholders to building meaningful relationships with them and staying attuned to their evolving circumstances and views. We also want our stakeholders to feel comfortable reaching out to us and to alert us to any changes that may impact us or our business. Ideally, they become allies, and even partners. When Hubert Joly got up close to Best Buy's stakeholders, both inside and outside the company, he began the process of establishing links with them to understand their perspectives. He also formed strong, meaningful bonds with many of them.

Deeper bonds are essential to understanding others' perspectives through our lenses. They increase trust, which allows stakeholders to be more honest with us and increases the quality of the information they share—which we collect through our outer lens. At the same time, a better honed inner lens based on courageous curiosity makes us more likely to seek out these types of bonds to begin with.

One particularly critical link Hubert forged was with key stakeholder Dick Schulze, Best Buy's founder. Recall that Schulze was attempting to regain control of the company. The battle between him and the board had become public, and some of the coverage was pretty bruising, such as a *Forbes* article titled, "See Dick Get No Respect: Why Best Buy's Founder Is Fighting for His Company."[5] Hubert recalled, "A company fighting with its founder seemed crazy to me."[6] What's more, he felt great admiration for Schulze. So he did something extraordinary.

Hubert prioritized going to meet Schulze in his first month on the job, making an appointment to visit him in the office of the foundation he was running. What's more, he showed Schulze great respect. "I entered Dick's office, wearing a suit and tie," Joly recalls, "and handed him my résumé. 'Under normal circumstances, you would have interviewed me,' I explained. 'So, I wanted to introduce myself properly.' Dick later told me that my gesture had touched him."[7]

That gesture, in fact, made great sense. It was an expression of wonderful humility, and it helped set a positive tone for their meeting. They were quickly able to amicably exchange views. Hubert shared the emerging strategy for turning Best Buy around, and Schulze could see that Hubert's map regarding the company's future and his own map overlapped. The beginnings of a strong relationship were forged.

As Hubert shares,

> Dick and I couldn't have been more different: He had spent his entire life building a retail business, and I had no retail experience. He knew Best Buy inside out, and I was an outsider. Still, we managed to find common ground. He was simply worried about the trajectory of the business he had built and wanted to do something about it. I shared with him some of my basic philosophies about people and customers. I also shared that I had no intention of blindly slashing stores or head count, both of which I considered Best Buy's great strengths. By the end of our conversation, the ice had been broken.[8]

A month later, Hubert visited Schulze at his home in Florida and they, along with Hatim Tyabji, the chairman of Best Buy's board at the time, continued discussing what they agreed and disagreed on regarding the company's future. Schulze told Hubert that should the attempt to take Best Buy private succeed, he would retain Hubert as CEO. In the end, Schulze wasn't able to secure the financing for making a takeover bid. The twist is that Hubert asked him to rejoin the company as chairman emeritus. Hubert wanted to deepen their relationship and continue to benefit from his advice.

Even more surprisingly, Hubert also established close, strong, and ongoing relationships with Best Buy's large consumer electronics vendors, including Microsoft, Samsung, and Apple. Many observers had predicted these vendors would run Best Buy out of business because they were opening their own stores. Hubert met with them and perceived that they actually had complementary interests. He proposed that Best Buy create "mini stores" within its stores for each of the brands, which would allow them to decide how they featured their products. They would have literally overlapping territory within Best Buy stores, representing a convergence of both companies' strategic maps.

In a short time, Hubert made a deal for the arrangement with Samsung, and by the end of his first year, the company had opened fourteen hundred Samsung mini stores within Best Buy locations. Other suppliers, including Microsoft, Sony, LG, and Google, followed suit, creating or expanding partnerships with Best Buy.[9] These partnerships proved to be a great success.

Hubert even found common ground with a key competitor, Amazon. He met with Amazon founder Jeff Bezos repeatedly, and in 2018, Best Buy sealed a deal to become the exclusive seller of smart TVs with Amazon's Fire TV streaming technology built in—securing sole distribution rights for nearly a dozen models of the product. Said Jeff Bezos of the arrangement, "A TV is a considered purchase . . . People do want to come in and see the TV. They want to experiment with the TV—try it out . . . Physical stores aren't going anywhere . . . E-commerce is going to be a part of everything, but not the whole thing." Jeff told Hubert that the "trust that their teams had built working together over the previous years had been essential to his decision to partner so closely."[10]

The Gift of Common Ground

We've found that when you want to establish a meaningful link with others, a great way to begin is to look for any common ground you can discover. Connection often begins with the small things we share: a sport or hobby, a place we've visited, or a familiar experience. Starting with these simple commonalities helps break the ice, and before long, people feel comfortable opening up.

The same principle applies in music. When you watch a jazz ensemble improvising on a piece of music—soaring far outside the notes written on the page in front of them—you might think that each of the players is off in their own little world, doing their own thing and making up their own rules as they go. And while "doing your own thing" is part of the magic of improvisation, if the players want to create a harmonious new version of a song, they have to find common ground and play within an agreed-to set of parameters.

Few understand this better than Wynton Marsalis, widely considered to be one of the greatest jazz musicians of all time, winner of nine Grammy Awards and a Pulitzer Prize, his jazz composition being the first ever to earn this distinction. He's been called "the Pied Piper of Jazz," and in addition to being a composer, music instructor, and bandleader, he serves as managing and artistic director of Jazz at Lincoln Center, director of jazz studies at The Juilliard School, and president of the Louis Armstrong Educational Foundation.

In an interview, Wynton explains,

> I think the one thing that makes jazz improvisation possible is the agreement. So, you have a lot of room to do different things, but you have to agree on the rhythm. If I'm playing in a rhythm and you're playing in a totally different rhythm, we're not going to agree. And not only are we not going to agree,

> we're not going to sound good. And if we don't have the same understanding of what we are trying to do on the bandstand, we're going to have a hard time.[11]

Sometimes you can find common ground easily, in obvious places. You learn you're from the same state, maybe both "Cornhuskers," a fond nickname for people from Nebraska. It's also the name of the football team of the Big Ten school, University of Nebraska-Lincoln. You may discover you're both big fans of the team, and you're off and running with memories of favorite plays or views of the current coach. If we're on the lookout for these common interests and experiences, and show a little curiosity, we can find them all over the place: You attended the same college, you love playing pickleball, or you prefer taking leisurely vacations on cruise ships.

In other cases, discovery will take more ingenuity.

Terry Szuplat, who served as a speechwriter for former President Barack Obama from 2009 to 2017, found himself in a predicament while on a trip in Australia. Obama was preparing to address several thousand Australian and American troops, but his speech was missing a crucial element: a strong opening. Running out of time, Szuplat was struggling to come up with an opener while in the motorcade.

Szuplat explained his problem to the burly, middle-aged Australian driver of their staff van. Without hesitation, the driver offered a simple solution: "No problem, mate. Obama should say, 'Aussie! Aussie! Aussie!'" Szuplat was initially confused, asking what would happen next, and the driver explained that everyone would yell back, "Oi! Oi! Oi!" Though unsure if the crowd would respond, he heard the driver confidently assure him, "Trust me, mate, they will."

A short while later, Obama stood before the troops with then Australian Prime Minister Julia Gillard. He began his speech by acknowledging, "I know that you all have a great Australian cheer," and then proceeded with the driver's suggestion: "Aussie! Aussie! Aussie!" As predicted, the crowd roared back, "Oi! Oi! Oi!" and burst out in smiles. With this simple act, Obama had established a personal connection with them.[12]

Of course, Obama shortly took off for more of his trip, but his openness to doing the chant speaks volumes about why he was so adept at building bonds with people all around the world.

Obama was lucky that his speechwriter had the presence of mind to seek the input of the driver and that the driver shared such a great idea. Sometimes you'll have to do a fair amount more exploring to uncover common ground, and you'll find it in places that surprise you.

In a TED Talk, global consumer strategist and Boston Consulting Group (BCG) Managing Director and Partner Aparna Bharadwaj discussed the hidden connections that transcend borders and defy stereotypes. Aparna was born in India but grew up in Iran, and she tells the story of watching celebrations for the festival of Nowruz when she was eight years old and how they reminded her of a similar festival, Lohri, in India that was also celebrated around a bonfire. Says Aparna, "Even an eight-year-old child can tell how profoundly similar those two events look in two sets of countries that are culturally so different. Like a kind of hidden connection."[13]

These hidden connections were a gift of common ground that gave Aparna comfort, much like the common ground of basic human needs and emotions Cornelia found across cultures, hierarchies, and professions as she moved from Minneapolis to Seoul to Barcelona and so on. She noticed a similar need for sharing warm moments in a community (as Aparna had experienced in Iran and India)—first in her own loneliness upon moving to Seoul, then with her classmates when starting boarding school and college, and even from leaders across industries who are lonely at the top. Cornelia felt an immediate connection with Aparna as she listened to her story, and was reminded that genuine connection, wherever it's found, is what allows leaders to find common ground across stakeholder groups.

The focus of Aparna's TED Talk was consumer habits in different regions and countries around the world, and the hidden similarities that she and her BCG team found when they looked at the data gathered from more than forty thousand consumers in eighteen countries. In one example, Aparna and her team found that Chinese people snack in a very specific way. They often buy their snacks hot and freshly prepared from a street vendor or at a food court, and they share them with others as a social indulgence. But what they found when they compared this consumer behavior with other countries was a surprise: People in countries with dramatically different cultures—such as Indonesia and Saudi Arabia—exhibited similar patterns.

Never assume you can't find common ground even with people from the most seemingly different life experiences and perspectives.

A Foundation of Trust in Connecting with Stakeholders

Late one night in a hospital emergency room, Sam, severely injured and in a "psychotic state," was screaming and yelling, holding a nurse, Sheila, hostage with a pair of scissors to her throat. George Kohlrieser, who was then a rookie hostage negotiator, was sent into this incredibly tense environment to defuse it.

Maintaining his composure, George calmly began by asking Sam, "What do you need, Sam? What do you want?" and "How can we help you right now?" In addition to Sam's continued screaming, he made a terrifying cut to the skin on Sheila's throat, then charged at George, scissors pointed at his throat, screaming threats to kill everyone.

Unflustered, George placed his hands on Sam's arms, and knowing from his briefing about Sam's children, focused on this critical connection point, asking, "What about your children, Sam?"

Sam's initial reply was a chilling threat to kill his children if they were brought there, yet George found encouragement in this, as it was Sam's first direct response. George then powerfully posed the question, "Do you want your children to remember you as a murderer?" A profound pause followed, and Sam's aggressive energy visibly shifted, signaling that George had found a way to connect with him.

George continued to guide the conversation, gradually calming Sam. Then he successfully negotiated for Sheila's release.

But he wasn't done yet. In a remarkable display of trust building, George then offered Sam choices regarding the scissors: "Would you throw them on the floor or hand them to me?" Sam chose to hand the weapon directly to George. As they walked out together, Sam sincerely thanked George, explaining, "For reminding me how important my children are to me."[14]

This harrowing experience highlights how creating a sense of safety and finding common ground, in this case a common humanity, can lead to breakthroughs in connecting with even the most extreme stakeholders. To give others the space to connect and explore new ways of thinking, we need to first make them feel secure.

George Kohlrieser, now a professor of leadership and organizational behavior at the International Institute for Management Development, uses an insightful mountain climbing metaphor in leadership development: A belayer who manages a climber's safety rope serves as a secure base—standing ready to catch them if they fall while providing them with the assurance they need to explore new areas and climb higher.

This closely parallels the psychological safety that Amy Edmondson describes as essential to organizations that are trying to thrive in a complex world where "nearly everything we value . . . is the result of decisions and actions that are interdependent." The solution, she explains, is an environment where people feel safe to share openly. "In a psychologically safe workplace people are not hindered by interpersonal fear. They feel willing and able to take the inherent interpersonal risks of candor. They fear holding back their full participation more than they fear sharing a potentially sensitive, threatening, or wrong idea."[15]

As leaders, we need secure relationships to give us the confidence to move from pessimistic fear to optimistic fear: the courage to face what scares us, using fear as a motivator to explore possibilities, find solutions, and move forward with purpose.

In Leaders' Circles, members offer one another that same level of assurance, opening their inner lenses and their willingness to learn from their peers. Within this safe space, they use their curiosity to explore new ways to see their environment and solve their problems.

In one of Cornelia's circles, four leaders—from Africa, Europe, North America, and South America—seemed initially to share little in common beyond their senior roles. But as they talked, they quickly discovered they were all facing the same challenge: After advancing to senior leadership positions, they realized that strong execution alone was no longer enough for further advancement. Personal branding and self-promotion, skills many find uncomfortable, were now essential as competition for the top roles intensified.

They each said in their own way, "This is a heavy lift," "It's not in my nature," "We need a solution," and "Let's see if we can crack this together." As it became clear to them that they all faced the same problem, they bonded in an instant.

This commonality wove threads of connection that soon extended across all eight leaders within their circle. Throughout our meetings, they used their connection and trust to create a *high quality of contact*, allowing them to honestly share their thoughts as they tackled their thorniest challenges together.

Creating a High Quality of Contact

Often, convincing others of our sincerity in wanting to form bonds with them will require an ongoing demonstration of our commitment. This challenge grows with the level of distrust people feel about your intentions or the magnitude of the divide or social distance between you, such as in the hierarchy of a company. The closer you are to the top, the harder it is to enjoy a higher quality of contact and connect authentically with your employees.

Alan Mulally knew that when you're interested in your employees, and you truly see them, it cuts down the social distance, and they'll open up. That's why he made it a habit to show up at the Ford cafeteria. If he'd done it just once or twice a year, many of the employees he talked with would've been too nervous to give him their honest opinions. Their thoughts would instantly scramble, and they'd fumble their words in the presence of their boss's boss's boss. However, because he made regular visits, gaining familiarity and trust, Alan established links with employees that became strong ropes of connection over time.

One great example of how his message effectively got through to employees is of an engineer, James Morgan, who took Alan at his word that he wanted people to share issues with him. When James appeared at Alan's office with his arms full of engineering schematics to share with him, Alan did something that many CEOs would never do. He invited him in for a conversation.

Looking through the schematics, Alan understood something about the lack of engineering discipline at Ford, and he saw a golden opportunity to reduce inefficiency in the company. Alan put James in charge of reducing complexity in their engineering process, and James became instrumental in Ford's engineering transformation and overall turnaround.[16] This kind of high quality of contact, built upon trust and connection, allows us to create meaningful, lasting relationships with our stakeholders. It also allowed Alan to benefit from deep insights that people at his level are rarely privy to.

Building high-quality bonds often requires an open mind and dedicated effort, but the rewards can far outweigh the investment. Cornelia was reminded of this when she got the idea of taking her mother for dinner at the famous El Bulli restaurant. This was in 2000—she was living in Paris and her mother would be visiting later that year. She called the restaurant for a reservation three months in advance.

The representative from El Bulli had a quick response: "Sorry, but we are completely booked. Try another time."

Cornelia followed this advice, and every time, the answer was the same: "Sorry, but we are completely booked. But you can call again another time." So she did just that. She continued to call regularly over the next three months, following the team's advice each time.

As the weeks went by, the calls felt less like routine exchanges and more like conversations. The voice on the other end began to carry a touch of warmth and they started to share a few moments of laughter. They didn't know each other's names, but a quiet sense of connection started to grow between them.

The day came when Cornelia and her mother were finally in town for their holiday in Roses, a lovely Spanish town near El Bulli. They still didn't have a reservation, but decided to try one last time. "Is there room for a reservation today?" After a few moments of silence, while she wondered if the person who answered had hung up the phone, the line came back to life.

"Yes, come at 8:00 p.m."

This time, it was Cornelia who fell silent. As the realization sank in that she and her mother would have the opportunity to finally meet the team and experience the extraordinary creativity of El Bulli firsthand that evening, she was filled with a feeling of overwhelming joy and gratitude. "Thank you so much. We'll see you soon," she answered.

Instead of going to the beach, they dropped off their bags, hailed a taxi, and set off for the restaurant. The ride took them along a winding road through the Catalonian hills, with sweeping views of the Mediterranean Sea, until they reached what looked like an isolated house beside a small parking lot. Still full of gratitude and excitement, they knocked on the door and were ushered into the restaurant by the host with a warm welcome.

Before being seated in the dining room, they were guided into a small room with three large viewing holes carved out of the wall. From their vantage point, they could see the sea almost as if they were sitting in front of it and feel the breeze. Although she'd never been there before, having been in touch with the restaurant so many times, the people, the welcome, and the venue already felt familiar.

When they were seated in the dining room, she realized that a special effort had been made to graciously accommodate her and her mother that day—a little table and chair had been added to the end of a long banquette where many of the diners were seated.

The entire experience was just as extraordinary as she had hoped. The unexpected ingredients, imaginative presentation, thoughtful staff, and serene atmosphere were truly unforgettable. After dinner, Cornelia asked the host whether their taxi had arrived to take her and her mother back to town.

"I'm sorry," was the response. "We forgot. I'll call right now. In the meantime, could we offer you a personal tour of the kitchen and an Armagnac as our guest?" Touched by the sincerity of their host's gesture, Cornelia and her mother gratefully accepted the offer, and their once-in-a-lifetime adventure continued.

Throughout the evening, Cornelia was struck not only by El Bulli's creativity, but by its spirit of generosity and care. What began as a string of polite but unsuccessful phone calls had turned into a lasting memory of the unexpected rewards of genuine human connection—an example of how a high quality of contact can make any organization truly exceptional.

High-quality business partnerships, founded on trust, give leaders a secure foundation to innovate and explore new opportunities together. When Netflix CEO Reed Hastings hired Ted Sarandos in 2000 to help expand its content offerings, Netflix was still a small company compared to today, with about $36 million in revenue in 2000. Sarandos went on to lead the extraordinarily successful growth of Netflix's DVD business and then its content streaming and original programming.

Based on their trusting relationship, Hastings formed a remarkable partnership with Sarandos, even serving as co-CEO with him. A study published in *Harvard Business Review* found that "nearly 60 percent of the companies led by co-CEOs outperformed," generating an average annual shareholder return of 9.5 percent—"significantly better than the average of 6.9 percent for each company's relevant index."[17]

Hastings called this "a high-performance technique. It's not for most situations and most companies. But if you've got two people that work really well together and complement, extend and trust each other, then it's worth doing."[18]

The Power of High-Quality Relationships

When Diane started a new role as the CEO of a struggling company, she quickly realized that the biggest obstacle wasn't its strategy. It was how disconnected the leaders had become from one another.

Within her first few weeks, she met with people from different levels of the organization, including all the members of her executive team. Through these conversations, she saw that the company was suffering from deeply siloed operations. The previous CEO had led with a command-and-control style—making all the decisions himself, with little exchange of ideas among his team—and that had translated into minimal coordination between departments.

Revenues were far below their potential, and Diane determined that this lack of alignment was at the root of the problem. To remedy this, she worked with her executive team to create a new operating structure, which they crafted together in an intensive, six-hour meeting. She also reached out to Cornelia for guidance on rebuilding trust and collaboration within her team.

Together, they replicated Cornelia's Leaders' Circle model within the company, bringing together senior leaders from different departments—for example, operations, legal, engineering, marketing, finance, and sales—to build relationships in small cross-functional circles. They also brought together departments that had historically clashed or had little familiarity with one another.

Cornelia began by asking these senior leaders to reintroduce themselves through stories about moments that had shaped their values throughout their lives. This broke the ice and gave everyone a greater sense of connection and understanding and a higher quality of contact. She then invited each leader to explain to their circle how they saw their role within the company and to share both the challenges and opportunities it faced.

Next, came a powerful exercise. Each person switched seats within the circle, taking the place of another leader. For example, the head of marketing moved to the head of sales' chair, and described that sales role as they understood it, including the pressures and opportunities they believed it had. After several rounds of switching seats—and with greater self-awareness about themselves and their roles—the leaders reconvened to collectively address challenges, identify opportunities to improve operations, and strengthen cross-departmental alignment.

Through the process, they gained deeper insight into their relationships with one another and into how each department's work impacted the rest of the organization. They developed a genuine appreciation for each other's perspectives and the pressures each leader was feeling from other departments. Together, they formed powerful bonds of understanding, connected the dots to find new solutions to longstanding, paralyzing problems, and gained a panoramic understanding of the organization, filling in their collective blind spots. They developed their relational lenses individually and as a team, which allowed them to learn more from each other than they could have in their silos. Together, they began to see new areas of the corporate landscape.

The turnaround started immediately. By the end of Diane's first year, the company's profit margin had grown by double digits as a result of increased coordination, reduced inefficiencies, and new initiatives.

Making High-Quality Connection a Norm

What Diane achieved with her leadership team can be scaled across an entire organization. To foster consistent and meaningful exchange of information, leaders should make sharing perspectives the norm.

This can start with the senior leadership team and eventually extend throughout the organization.

Alan Mulally achieved this at Ford through a process he'd implemented with his executive team at Boeing, called the business plan review (BPR), a mandatory weekly meeting for senior executives. This meeting facilitated continuous sharing of problems the executives faced, learnings about them, and effective solutions to these problems. It also forged powerful bonds of trust and support among the executives.

We love the story about how Ford's executives first reacted to his weekly business plan reviews. The review process required each executive to present a status report with the progress of key goals highlighted in red, yellow, or green. Alan included a broader group of executives than had formerly come to executive team meetings. He recalls,

> The business plan review meeting was led by me every week for a few hours with the entire senior leadership team. I included every major discipline—engineering, manufacturing, procurement, government, community relations, all the suppliers, everybody. So, once a week, we would go through everything about the vision, the strategy, and the plan.[19]

For the first few meetings, every single executive who attended gave their projects a green rating, hiding the true turmoil in their departments—there wasn't a yellow or red to be seen. Given the company's dire situation, Alan knew that couldn't be the case. He pointedly said, "You guys, we're going to lose $17 billion this year. Is there just anything, one little thing that's not going well?"[20]

The executives got the message loud and clear. Only a few months after Alan arrived at Ford, one brave soul, Mark Fields, reported the very first red during a business plan review, the delayed launch of the Ford

Edge in Canada due to unresolved problems with the car's suspension. Alan asked if anyone could help him with the problem. Another executive said he could, and with that assistance, Mark was able to resolve the issue.

This example showed the executives how helpful they could be to one another, and it set a powerful model of openness and connection for the rest of the organization. If Mark hadn't been honest and shown red for the Ford Edge launch, those connections might never have been made, and executives may have continued to miss the opportunity to collaborate and support each other. Beyond the green, yellow, and red traffic light system of coding, what truly mattered was the leaders' shared commitment to openness—freely contributing their experience and ideas to help one another overcome challenges.

The power of building and maintaining meaningful bonds and high-quality relationships with others cannot be overemphasized. Every stakeholder connection you make increases the breadth of your vision as a panoramic leader and widens your outer lens. Ultimately, it's through shared understanding, the courageous act of finding common ground with those around you, and the consistent effort to build trust that true leadership emerges.

We can never allow complacency to creep into our worldview. The world continues to change around us, and, like explorers sailing to uncharted lands, we must constantly adjust our maps accordingly. In the next chapter, we explore the most effective ways to keep your map up to date.

As you focus on establishing meaningful bonds with your stakeholders, here are some questions that will help you focus on what's most important.

QUESTIONS TO CONSIDER

- When was the last time I learned something surprising from a stakeholder? What made that possible?
- Who are the "unlikely associates" in my life with whom I can find common ground to create partnerships?
- Are there any dormant stakeholder relationships that need revitalizing?
- What fears of the unknown or of leaving my comfort zone are holding me back, and who or what can I rely on as a secure base?
- How can I shift from pessimistic fear to optimistic fear and deepen bonds with stakeholders?
- What regular practices can I institute in my personal or professional life to ensure that high-quality connection becomes the norm?

CHAPTER 7

Step 3: Map Your Evolving Perspective

The art of mapmaking was revolutionized during World War I, in great part to keep up with the constant tunneling of new trenches along the Western Front. The Allies and Central Powers both dug extensive networks of trenches, separated by a narrow span of desolate No Man's Land. Generally only a few feet wide, the trenches were just deep enough for soldiers to stand up in without the tops of their heads being exposed. Snipers on both sides maintained a vigilant watch, ready to fire at the slightest movement above the trench line when a soldier, out of necessity or momentary lapse, risked a glance over the parapet for a view of the world outside the cramped and fetid confines.

As soldiers continuously extended the trenches, they created elaborate webs, which ultimately stretched about 475 miles, from the coast of the English Channel to the Swiss border.[1] Mapping the ever-elongating and winding tendrils was essential but extremely dangerous work, and the British, French, German, and other armies developed innovative, remarkable processes to multiply their effectiveness.

The British military, among others, combined mapping by surveyors on land with aerial photographs. The reconnaissance aircraft would fly over the trenches while a photographer in the plane's back seat would point the camera down at the target below, leaning over the side and into the cold slipstream. These soon evolved into floor-mounted cameras that could be triggered midflight, capturing and mapping miles of terrain.[2]

They captured overlapping frames of the same terrain, which mapmakers then merged into a single continuous representation of the area. That would then be combined with the maps made by the land surveyors. By the end of the war, more than 34 million maps of the Western Front had been created by the United Kingdom alone.[3]

Align Your Map with Others' Using Landmarks

The first two steps in improving our panoramic leadership, which we've covered in chapters 5 and 6—getting up close to stakeholders and establishing meaningful bonds—are designed to help you understand and strengthen relationships so that you can gather a panoramic range of perspectives. The question then becomes, what do we do with them? How do we use them to chart new areas of our maps, add valuable detail, and then reflect these insights back out to our stakeholders?

In this chapter, we'll answer these questions by describing a process for applying these perspectives to your own map: First, align your map with others' using landmarks. Then, compare the maps to see where they converge and where they differ, and how they fit together to reveal the broader landscape. Finally, expand or modify your existing map by integrating relevant insights. Let's start with the first step.

You might be wondering how the World War I mapmakers knew what to change or add onto their base maps given the new aerial photographs and land surveys they were getting. They first aligned the new photos with their existing maps using familiar landmarks or reference points, such as hedgerows, clusters of trees, or other control points. Then they could pinpoint the changes in trenches they needed to add.

Like those World War I cartographers, to effectively incorporate others' perspectives into our own maps, we need to begin by aligning our maps using landmarks or reference points to see where they overlap and where they're different. How do we find those landmarks? We can begin by using the topic of discussion as a landmark.

In Cornelia's peer circles, when a leader brings up a dilemma, their topic becomes a landmark for other leaders in their circle, anchoring the discussion so they can consult their maps and share their own experiences that relate to it. As the group explores ideas and possible solutions together, offering new perspectives with that landmark as a reference point, the leader presenting the dilemma sees more context and options—more of the landscape around their dilemma. At the same time, peers also add what they learn from the discussion to *their* maps, modifying or building onto their existing insights on the topic.

When you gather input from your full panorama of stakeholders—like layering aerial photos from the Western Front onto your existing map—start by identifying overlapping interests, experiences, and goals. For example, both your engineering and design teams might recommend discontinuing a product—even if it still has loyal customers—because they believe their time would be better spent focusing on newer offerings. These two teams can use the idea of a new product as a landmark and bring parts of their maps together.

Sometimes, you have to create these reference points for your stakeholders. When Alan Mulally took over as CEO of Ford, he created—on a company-wide scale—a shared understanding about the values and behaviors that would guide all employees in their work. The Our "Working Together"© Leadership and Management System principles and practices brought that shared understanding to life. Most fundamental were the principles of "People first . . . Love 'em up," "Everyone is included," and "Compelling vision, comprehensive strategy, and relentless implementation."

As Alan reflected on the power of these principles, "What is so surprising about "Working Together" is that it's not complicated; it is in its essence an adaptation of timeless human values to the modern business world. That's why it was embraced by employees and brought the teams together; it was familiar at a basic human level. It represents the values that we all share, principles that are ancient and embedded in our DNA."[4]

Alan constantly reinforced the importance of the "Working Together" principles and practices in creating a vision and strategy that would involve all stakeholders and benefit each one. During his time at Ford, everyone knew the vision and strategy and the progress being made, as the outcomes of the business plan review meetings were widely distributed. Alan shared in an interview, "Everything that we look at is flowed throughout the organization, out through all of the stakeholders, and then the data is updated and flows all the way back up. Then we communicate it to everybody."[5]

We often have an easier time aligning our maps if we're all working with common principles, practices, and a shared understanding. Just as Alan introduced the "Working Together" principles as guidelines for how people should bring their maps together, you can introduce principles and practices within your own team—or across an entire organization—to build the kind of alignment that made Ford so successful under Alan's leadership.

Having aligned our maps by identifying common landmarks, the next step is to explore where they converge and where they diverge. Differences aren't drawbacks. In fact, they're often the source of deeper understanding.

Exploring Differences Across Maps

Not every part of your maps will line up, and that's precisely what makes them valuable. Differing, even contradictory, insights reveal nuances on your map, helping you zoom in on areas that deserve closer attention and identify new opportunities. For instance, let's return to the previous example of the engineering and design teams eager to prioritize new products. Now let's say a sales representative in the field notices growing nostalgia for the product you've been advised to discontinue. Instead of cutting it outright, you might look more closely and discover an opportunity to grow it for a limited time by marketing it as a beloved vintage item.

For panoramic leaders, differing perspectives are the raw material of better judgment. They help us sort through the information we collect, clarify priorities, and anticipate risks. They test assumptions and reveal how various stakeholders' perspectives can be integrated into a coherent picture. For example, a new strategic initiative may offer exceptional potential but carry significant risk. Examining this tension can reveal opportunities to support the bold move while managing downsides to a sustainable level.

By engaging with conflicting views productively, leaders uncover blind spots, refine their priorities, and navigate growing complexity with sounder judgment. Cornelia sees this process unfold constantly in her Leaders' Circles, just as Marshall sees it among the leaders he coaches—each finding that real growth comes from exploring differences, not avoiding them.

A client of Marshall's was caught in a storm of frustration and stagnation as mounting tensions flared between the marketing and product development teams. Marketing, driven by an urgent need for aggressive campaigns to boost sales, clashed with product development, which worried about the feasibility and long-term sustainability of delivering on those promises. The conflict had created a crippling bottleneck, hindering growth. A crucial first step was encouraging leaders on both sides to acknowledge the genuine validity of each other's concerns and recognize that both perspectives were essential to success.

The pathway to resolution involved workshops designed specifically to allow both teams to candidly discuss their priorities and their very real challenges. The goal was to build empathy and shift focus from defensive agendas to shared objectives. Gradually, by exploring their different perspectives, the teams saw that their seemingly conflicting goals were not mutually exclusive but complementary—the very difference that made them stronger. Together, they cocreated an adaptable, realistic road map that aligned marketing strategies with product capabilities while addressing the risks and constraints they faced. The process resolved the immediate conflict, strengthened collaboration, and laid the foundation for a winning solution built on a realistic strategy and innovative product enhancements.

This kind of collaboration reflects the deeper work of panoramic leadership, where differences in perspective become sources of clarity and insight. From here, we can continue to microtranslate, or interpret between the maps of multiple stakeholders to reinforce similarities and reveal greater detail where they diverge, allowing us to see the landscape more completely, much like skilled navigators have done for centuries.

Interpreting and Translating: Combining Maps

Historians tell us that beginning more than a thousand years ago, the Polynesians explored ten million square miles of the Pacific Ocean—an area stretching from Hawaii to Easter Island to New Zealand, the vast "Polynesian Triangle." And they accomplished all this without any of the navigational instruments European explorers used. Instead, they sharpened and applied the tools they already had inside of them—the ability to be highly attuned to a bird in flight, an ocean swell, the position of stars, the rising and setting of the sun, the direction of the wind, or a cloud hovering in the sky. These signs and many others in the environment told them everything they needed to know to succeed.

In the previous chapter, we learned that Tupaia sailed with Captain Cook through Polynesia. As they sailed together, the two men were able to combine their complementary knowledge of sailing and cartography—each expanding their personal map with the perspective of the other.

Tupaia's highly accurate, traditional Polynesian navigational skills profoundly impressed the captain. Cook himself wrote, "These people sail in those Seas from Island to Island for several hundred Leagues, the Sun serving them for a Compass by day, and the Moon and Stars by night."[6] Science writer and geneticist Cristy Gelling observes of Tupaia, "He amazed the sailors by correctly pointing in the direction of Tahiti, even after they had sailed around New Zealand and up the east coast of Australia to Indonesia. Cook was particularly intrigued by Tupaia's claim to know the way to some 130 islands."[7]

At Cook's request to draw as many islands as he knew, Tupaia created a map he hoped Cook would understand—drawing, according to some experts, seventy-four islands and providing their names.

Suggests Gelling, "For Cook, a map was a bird's-eye view of the curved world stretched onto a two-dimensional plane. Tupaia instead took a canoe's-eye view, a perspective that shifts depending on where you start from." That wasn't the only difference. While Europeans like Cook would have north at the top of the map, it's believed that Tupaia put it in the center of the map.[8]

The world Cook came from was one where science ruled. Navigation was primarily accomplished using a combination of instruments such as sextants, compasses, chronometers, and nautical charts. Armed with these tools, Captain Cook and his crew circumnavigated the world, charting the new lands they discovered with remarkable precision.

The world Tupaia came from was much different. He measured the distance between islands not by the physical space between them but by the time it took to get from one to another, which was affected by factors such as the trade winds and swells in the ocean. Consistent with oral tradition, the maps were stored in the mind and passed on from generation to generation through years of apprenticeship. Each steeped in their own cultures and traditions, Cook and Tupaia brought together two completely different styles of mapmaking, and thus different ways of seeing the world.

To combine the elements of their maps, they had to microtranslate for each other—adapting learning from one context so it could be applied in another—much as the peers in Cornélia's Leaders' Circles help one another to see their different perspectives.

To understand the European approach, Tupaia had to learn to see the traditional Polynesian time measurements between islands as physical distances. For the European navigators to understand Tupaia's cartography, they had to imagine themselves on their ship at a starting location, say in a bay of one of the islands. They then had to draw two imaginary lines in their minds—the first from where they stood on the ship to the sun where it would be at its zenith, at noon. The second line followed the path the Polynesians would take to get to their destination island. They would then measure the angle between those two lines, clockwise down from the sun, which played the role of the northernmost point of a compass.[9]

For example, on Tupaia's first map, the angle between a certain island in the Marquesas chain and O'ahu in the Hawaiian island chain was calculated by this means as 335 degrees. This measurement is phenomenally close to the 330 degrees NNW for the same calculation on a Western Mercator map.[10]

Through this process of combining their maps, Tupaia and Cook each had to interpret the other's perspective—and also microtranslate their perspective for the other person. That process allowed them to create a much better collective understanding of this part of the world than each had understood on his own. The German naturalist Johann Reinhold Forster, who sailed aboard the *Resolution* on Cook's later voyage, praised the map as a "monument of ingenuity."[11]

Microtranslating between maps helps us move beyond *exploring* commonalities and differences to *combining* them in our mapmaking. It's one of the most rewarding parts of bringing our maps together, because it allows us to understand a more complete and accurate picture of our world—one that reveals far more than we could see on our own—including the unknown areas still waiting to be explored.

Filling In Your Blind Spots, Expanding Your Map

Over three hundred years after Cook and Tupaia set forth together, in July 2010, Captain Punua Tamaehu, a traditional Polynesian navigator, or wayfinder, led his crew on a traditional sailing boat, the *'O Tahiti Nui Freedom*, specially built for this occasion. They'd embarked on a nearly twenty-thousand-kilometer voyage, from Tahiti to China, as a tribute to their Polynesian ancestors who, starting six thousand years ago, had migrated eastward along the route. On the way, they stopped at the Tahitian island of Raiatea, the Cook Islands, Tonga, Fiji, Vanuatu, the Solomon Islands, Papua New Guinea, and the Philippines.

The historic boat held up well for the most part, at least until the crew ran into a fierce storm with intense wind and rain, leaving the sail so badly torn that it was virtually useless. The crew persisted, moving the boat slowly forward through ocean swells. At their slowed pace, their provisions wouldn't last, and while they could catch some fish, they were at increased risk of dehydration.

Pondering their predicament, Captain Punua found himself turning his reading glasses around and around in his hand before setting them down. As he looked down at them, he had a striking realization: A temple of his glasses—the long, thin part that goes behind the ear—could be fashioned into a needle for repairing the sail. He broke off one of the temples with a brisk "crack" and used a knife to sharpen one end to a fine point. Soon after, they were sailing at full speed again. Four months after leaving Tahiti, the *'O Tahiti Nui Freedom* entered the port of Fujian, greeted by a jubilant crowd, and then Shanghai, its final destination.

As Punua told Cornelia, "Perspectives and solutions are all around us, showing us the direction forward, whether it's the swells in the sea or the color of the clouds. Sometimes they're obvious to see, like the sun shining overhead, but at other times, the sun is barely visible. Like my glasses, the solution may be in your hands, but you may not see it if you don't look from the right angle."[12]

As we consider the input we get from our intelligence gathering, we have to be sure to look at our map from all angles—from the full panorama of our stakeholders. Input we might be inclined to dismiss can be vital to filling a blind spot.

At the back of the human eye is the retina, a structure that contains cells sensitive to light—rods and cones. It's these cells that gather images from the world around us and transmit them to our brain via the optic nerve, which is connected to the retina. That specific location where the optic nerve connects to the retina is called the *blind spot* because there are no light-sensitive cells there—you literally cannot see images projected on that specific piece of optical real estate.

Most of the time, you don't notice your blind spot. That's because your brain uses the context, or visual information from the area of the retina around the blind spot, and perspectives from the other eye, to fill in an image of what must be in the blind spot. We see so much more with two eyes than just one, because life isn't meant to be seen from just one perspective.

Just as your brain fills in your blind spot by using vision from both eyes, when you get observations from different stakeholders, you're much more likely to spot opportunities and navigate around obstacles. And through the work of interpreting and translating others' maps, we start to see more clearly where our own maps may be incomplete.

The next step is to expand our maps, filling in our blind spots and integrating new angles or perspectives into our landscape that change how we navigate forward. To get started, ask yourself whether you might be overlooking other perspectives. Then build on relationships you've formed with stakeholders in that blank space to build meaningful bonds—and test and expand your understanding.

Blind spots don't just affect how we see the world. They also shape how we try to *fill* them in. They influence how we interpret information and whose input we choose to trust. Our values, priorities, and loyalties can subtly distort what we consider to be important—and the same is true for our stakeholders. Recognizing these hidden influences in how we complete our maps is the first step toward truly integrating our stakeholders' perspectives and refining our shared understanding of reality.

A Deeper Understanding of Our Stakeholders—and Ourselves

When we're interpreting stakeholder perspectives, it's helpful to pause and reflect on something we often overlook: Our stakeholders have *their own* stakeholders. By deepening our understanding of the people and pressures that shape our stakeholders' maps, we can more easily recognize the constraints and priorities influencing their decisions. For example, this can help explain the disproportionate loyalties people sometimes feel toward their "silo" within an organization. If you work in R&D, you may see the manufacturing team as unreasonably resistant to improvements your colleagues believe would enhance the product. And if you don't make the effort to explore beyond that frustration, you may miss the operational realities they face. Changes that seem straightforward in concept may not be practical to produce or may increase costs beyond what customers will pay.

People rarely act in isolation. They're influenced by the interests and expectations of their own stakeholders. This issue was highlighted by Ronald Heifetz and Marty Linsky, professors at the Harvard Kennedy School, and Alexander Grashow in their book, *The Practice of Adaptive Leadership*:

> No stakeholders operate solo. They have external loyalties, to people outside their group and to the people behind the ideas that matter to them. When representatives from a teachers union enter a bargaining session, they intend to fight not only for their own interests but also for the interests of those they represent: the team members who selected them to go to the meeting, the union members and their families, their peers in other unions who have expectations of them, and the organization itself. All of these other parties are counting on the

> representatives to protect their jobs and provide them with some security so they can make the mortgage payments and have time for their own children as well. The representatives may also feel loyal to an idea about the role of unions. Perhaps they read a biography of the revered labor leader David Dubinsky twenty-five years ago in graduate school, or they worked with farm worker rights activist César Chavez the year after graduation. How could they ever let those icons down?[13]

Understanding our stakeholders' alliances helps us better interpret their behaviors and decisions—the reasons behind their choices and the context in which they make them—allowing us to see deeper into their maps. Their stakeholders influence their values, goals, and perspective on the best course of action. To continue the example of the union representative above, he may have a personal desire to come to an agreement and prefer to make certain concessions. But if union members are opposed, he likely won't make these concessions and might even choose to announce a strike because he feels he must prioritize loyalty to the union's members.

To identify our stakeholders' loyalties—and to see where they overlap with our own or with the loyalties of other stakeholders—we can ask questions like, Who are they trying to please? Whose input do they value or prioritize? How is that shaping their perspective?

As we evaluate what to add to our maps and what to leave out, we should also consider which loyalties of our *own* might be swaying our judgment. Some of these, as Heifetz, Linsky, and Grashow caution, may be "unspeakable loyalties," which are "the loyalties you have that are getting in the way of the goals you tell everyone about . . . Often these unspeakable loyalties come from some need, protection, or insecurity." An example they offer is an unwillingness to share our salaries because we believe people will be angry at how much we make, even if that silence erodes a fragile culture of transparency in our organization.[14]

Whether a company division, a country, or a family, each stakeholder group develops norms and expectations that shape how its members think and act. We need to be aware of how those influences shape our own judgment, and whether we consciously accept them. If we feel our decision conflicts with those established norms or expectations—even when we recognize the wisdom of that decision—we may still resist or abandon it, just as the union representative in our earlier example considered holding a strike.

To better understand how these influences affect us, the authors recommend we ask ourselves questions to identify our loyalties: "To whom do I feel most responsible? Who would react most vigorously if I did something out of the routine? Whom am I trying hardest to please or impress? Who would I most disappoint? Whose support do I most need?"[15]

Once you've assessed both your stakeholders' and your own loyalties, you'll be in a better position to use your relational lens and effectively integrate helpful parts of their perspectives into your map. As you do, you'll need to continue to interpret and translate by asking more questions to see the relationships between your maps. For instance, given the stakeholders' values, loyalties, and priorities, would they do things differently? Would they see alternatives that I don't? Does bringing our different perspectives together create new opportunities or a more productive strategy going forward? Does it help me see further and understand more about the world?

See the Whole So You Can See *from* the Whole

Each stakeholder's perspective is valid, yet no single group or stakeholder offers a complete view on its own. As we're reminded by the parable of the blind men and the elephant in chapter 1—where each man touches a different part of the elephant and mistakes it for the whole—real insight comes from bringing our stakeholders' maps together. Only then can we see the entire picture, especially through one another's eyes—and from the eyes of the elephant, or the whole organization.

A member of one of Cornelia's peer circles, David, led the Asia Pacific region for an international corporation. He faced an escalating conflict among his direct reports that was starting to spin out of control. Two of his five country managers were locked in a dispute that was rooted in historical tensions between their countries.

In meetings, they readily agreed to collaborate. Yet in the weeks that followed, communication broke down, and their tension began to spread through the team, threatening productivity and collaboration across the region.

Amy, a fellow leader in David's Leaders' Circle who'd lived on three continents, shared examples of rivalries she'd witnessed elsewhere that outlasted generations and continued to affect relationships among leaders. Listening to her, David realized that the problem wasn't simply a personal feud but the deeper influence of legacy and loyalties.

Other peers challenged him to reflect on his own leadership. He'd met with each country manager individually, but he hadn't built the trust that comes from bringing them together as a group. Cornelia offered the metaphor of the bicycle wheel. David was the hub; his relationship with each individual country manager was a spoke, but there were no direct lateral connections among the five managers independent of him to form the unified wheel that would move the organization forward.

These insights changed David's approach.

At the next regional event, he gathered the country managers together for a relaxed dinner. No agenda. David began by sharing stories about some of his stakeholders, including his family and his volunteer organization to support youth development. His openness set the tone, and soon the managers were sharing stories about their own stakeholders. As the evening unfolded, small but meaningful connections began to surface. One manager discovered that his adult child lived in the same city as another manager, and they agreed to meet during his next visit. Another revealed that he'd spent a year in California as an exchange student, where another manager had spent part of their childhood. What had once been a table of rivals began to feel like a circle of colleagues.

The impact spread beyond the dinner table. By the following week, they'd begun exchanging information essential to aligning their operations and bringing their maps together. Collaboration deepened as their own teams followed suit. By the end of the next quarter, trust had taken root, strengthening relationships, aligning goals, and setting a new standard for how the region worked together. The managers had moved beyond their individual maps to see the landscape through one another's eyes. By bringing their maps together, they were able to see the region as an interconnected whole rather than a collection of competing parts.

And when leaders shift their vantage point in this way, the entire organization begins to move as one.

Turning Perspective into Performance

Hubert Joly exemplified true panoramic leadership when he took the reins at the underperforming Best Buy in 2012—and began a major remapping for himself and for the company.

Through an open inner lens, he applied the hard-earned insights gained from his earlier transitions into new industries. He knew that real progress would require trusting others' expertise and allowing their perspectives to reshape his map. To widen his outer lens, he spent time in stores listening to a panoramic range of stakeholders, gaining critical insight into the retail industry and Best Buy's unique challenges. Through his relational lens, he didn't simply absorb what he heard. He brought those perspectives back to the leadership team, integrating them into a shared understanding of the company's future.

Sitting at a massive, U-shaped conference table, Hubert and about thirty leaders from across Best Buy collectively developed a turnaround strategy called Renew Blue just two months after he stepped into the CEO role. Rather than issuing a directive, he built the strategy with them—merging maps and turning diverse viewpoints into coordinated action. To build buy-in, Hubert then took the plan to the top 150 leaders in the company (the Best Buy Operating Council) before presenting what they "wanted to achieve for shareholders, but also for employees, customers, vendors, and the world around us" to the investment community.[16]

In addition to creating branded mini stores inside Best Buy locations, turning the company around involved enhancing the shopping experience by simplifying floor layouts to make products easier to find, ramping up space for the most popular items like mobile phones, improving the online shopping experience, developing stronger relationships with vendors, and large-scale cost reductions, among other initiatives.

Hubert's panoramic leadership—his ability to integrate a wide range of perspectives into a shared strategic direction—helped Best Buy move from a loss in 2013 to profitability the very next year. By the end of his second year as CEO, the company had solidly rebounded.

But Hubert didn't stop there. Rather than coast on the company's success, he launched a major initiative to look for new growth opportunities, creating a strategic growth office as part of the Building the New Blue strategy.[17] This office, which grew to about fifty people, emphasized initiative and experimentation, adding a stronger risk-taking mentality to the company's evolving map.

Even if you've achieved great success with your map, panoramic leadership does not end there. Each time you look outward, you'll see more opportunities, your map will expand again, and you'll be motivated to keep growing.

Never Stop Exploring

Our maps are never final. They continuously evolve as the world—and our own perspective—transforms amid today's accelerating pace of change. So even after we've updated our map with new understanding and discovered more opportunities to grow, solve problems, and create partnerships with our stakeholders, we need to keep exploring. To move forward, we must stay engaged with stakeholders, gather new insights, and continue connecting new dots.

As Best Buy evolved and grew, Hubert Joly expanded his own map once more, continuing the cycle of learning and renewal that lies at the heart of panoramic leadership. During the company's turnaround, his hands-on leadership style had been essential. But as the business regained its footing, he received feedback that it was time to step back. "I made lots of decisions fast," he recalls, "but now things were going well. We had an extraordinary team of highly talented people who respected and trusted each other. Decisions did not have to be made *by me* all the time."[18] Hubert saw that his career was a journey of continuous self-renewal. This was a crucial factor in the extraordinary results he achieved.

By the time he left Best Buy in the hands of a new leadership team in June 2019, the company's share price had more than tripled in value from when he took over.[19] The next year, in 2020, the company had earnings of $1.5 billion. He was named one of the one hundred "Best-Performing CEOs in the World" by *Harvard Business Review*, one of the top thirty CEOs in the world by *Barron's*, and one of the top ten CEOs in the United States in Glassdoor's annual Employees' Choice Awards.

While there is no definitive way to know which way the winds of change will blow, continuously revalidating and expanding our map through the GEM Process and clarifying what we perceive through our three lenses will stand us in strong stead. Just as some of the most successful CEOs developed this discipline, we must engage in regular, ongoing discussion with stakeholders, vigorously gather data, and adapt our map, reflecting our insight back out to stakeholders through our leadership. It's an efficient—and highly rewarding—process.

As you continue to explore and lead, here are some questions you can ask to facilitate the process.

QUESTIONS TO CONSIDER

- What key landmarks or reference points in my life help me orient myself and pinpoint changes in my personal map? In what ways do these landmarks enable me to integrate new experiences and insights?

- What common lesson am I repeatedly gaining from different stakeholders in my life, whether personal or professional? How am I actively factoring this learning into my personal map?
- Who are all the stakeholders relevant to my organization or a specific project I'm leading? What are their potentially competing interests, and how can I try to address them?
- How do my loyalties shape my blind spots and influence how I understand others' maps?
- What options might my stakeholders see that I don't, and how can bringing our perspectives together reveal further possibilities?
- How can I use my inner, outer, and relational lenses together—taking in new perspectives, turning them into insight, and sharing that insight—to align and energize others?

The GEM Process

Bringing together the three steps explored in part two, we've shaped them into a practical yet powerful framework we call the GEM Process—a guide to becoming a panoramic leader. The following charts illustrate how each step translates into individual actions, collective practices, and the skills that bring them to life.

The GEM Cycle

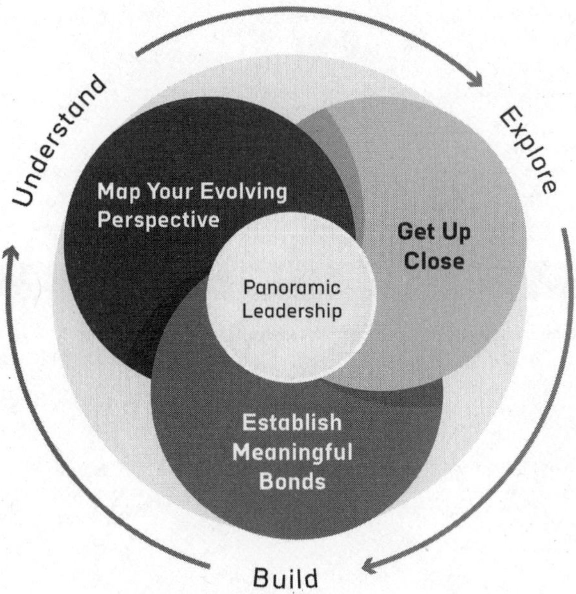

The Panoramic Leadership Framework

Leadership Lenses

GEM Process

	INNER LENS	RELATIONAL LENS	OUTER LENS
GET UP CLOSE (Explore)	• **Embrace uncertainty** • Interrupt autopilot • Check your assumptions	• **Widen your field of view** • Consider competing perspectives • Shift vantage points	• **Engage new stakeholders** • Look beyond the familiar • Ask: Who's not at the table?
ESTABLISH MEANINGFUL BONDS (Build)	• **Use courageous curiosity** • Find comfort in discomfort • Lean into optimistic fear	• **Find common ground** • See potential allies • Understand evolving views	• **Build lasting relationships** • Deepen trust • Elevate quality of contact
MAP YOUR EVOLVING PERSPECTIVE (Understand)	• **Revise your map** • Examine your loyalties • Resolve blind spots	• **Refract insights outward** • Reframe differences as assets • Translate between maps	• **Align stakeholders** • Identify landmarks to anchor exploration • Continue evolving shared understanding

CHAPTER 8

Three Principles for Making Panoramic Leadership Work

Sometimes, the best-laid business plans go astray. Marshall recalls the time two large pharmaceutical companies attempted to merge three times, unsuccessfully. Despite the potential benefits of the merger, the plan failed due to interpersonal disputes at the senior level.

Personality clashes, ego, and ambition kept the leaders from seeing their common ground—and blinded them to the fact that the merger was in both of their interests. This lack of alignment led to confusing chains of responsibility, chaotic attempts to combine their operations, and pushback from top executives who could have done a good deal to make things work. This story is all too common. One study of forty thousand mergers and acquisitions over the course of forty years found that 70–75 percent of them ultimately failed to achieve their strategic goals.[1]

We've witnessed more times than we can count that when executives roll out a big, new initiative—with all the brass bands, flashing lights, and hoopla—it often goes nowhere fast. Developing your panoramic leadership skills will go a long way to ensuring success with your initiatives, whether they're large-scale or more incremental.

In this chapter, we introduce three principles for optimizing your implementation of panoramic leadership. These three stakeholder-driven principles will help ensure you get your return on your investment of time and energy, and they'll allow you to push your organization forward in the way you need with clarity, focus, and alignment.

Don't work for the process—make it work for *you*. Focus on these priorities and make them your friends and constant companions.

Principle 1: Set Crystal-Clear Priorities

One of the people Marshall coaches was, until recently, a top administrator of a US federal government agency. Her list of accomplishments as a leader is as long as your arm—maybe longer. Yet, when she started working with Marshall, she shared, "Everybody's complaining because we don't have clear priorities. Well, we do have priorities, but the president of the United States calls and everything changes."

When the president of the United States calls and tells you to do something and have it on his desk in a week, what are you going to say? "I'm sorry; we're busy? This doesn't fit in our framework of priorities?" Absolutely not. You're going to change your priorities and deliver what's asked for, in a week if not sooner.

If you fail to set clear priorities, then with so many competing demands, *everything* becomes a priority. Which means that you won't really have priorities. All your teams will be doing is putting out fires.

During periods of rapid change, people do not need less structure in decision-making—they need more. That means creating a clear framework for the team on how to move forward. Doing so requires real discipline on your part. If something doesn't relate to a priority, put it on the back burner until it does come up. If an emergency occurs in your organization, then the first thing you must do is sit down with each of your direct reports, whether individually or all together as a team, and clearly reprioritize. By modeling this discipline, you signal to your team that you expect the same clarity and focus from them.

When Alan Mulally ran Boeing and then Ford, the priorities were always made clear, even throughout industry-disrupting events like 9/11 at Boeing and the 2008 financial crisis at Ford. His teams knew what information and inputs to pay attention to and which to put on their own back burners. They then shared those priorities with their teams and throughout the organization.

Principle 2: Get Priorities into Your Incentive Plan

One of Marshall's clients is the CEO and vice chairman of a multibillion-dollar international bank. One day, he said to his team, consisting of the top ten people in the bank: "We're spending too much time on short-term stuff. We're not thinking about the future. We're not looking outside the bank. We need to think bigger, right?"

After everyone nodded their heads in agreement, he made a very specific request: "I want you to spend four hours next week and do nothing but look outside the bank. Think long-term strategy, think big picture, for four hours next week."

Now, how many of these ten executives do you think followed through on the request?

Not a single one of them.

They all had reasons. "Well, I had an urgent crisis that I had to deal with."

"Something came up, and I didn't have time."

"I had other priorities to take care of first—I'll get to it soon."

And on and on.

Now, those were all legitimate demands on their time, but the CEO had been entirely clear about what he wanted from them—longer-term thinking. They didn't follow through on his request because the CEO hadn't connected this long-term task to what mattered to them—their compensation, recognition, or purpose.

Consider the plight of one of the bank's executive vice presidents. He was getting constantly hammered to improve the bank's numbers—it had been a tough year—and his compensation was tied directly to bottom-line results. No improvement, no bonus, and perhaps no job. The CEO was asking him to take four hours of his precious time to explore the long-term future of the bank, which would reduce the amount of time he was able to spend on improving that quarter's numbers, which according to his incentive structure could ultimately lead to a personal financial hit.

Make no mistake about it, this CEO is an immensely successful banking leader, and he has never had a problem ensuring that his executives' compensation was tied directly to achieving the company's goals. However, he never imagined that he'd have to make such a simple task an explicit part of his executives' incentives.

We know from our experience with leaders of all sorts that if you want your teams to do something that's even just a small step outside of their other priorities, you must tie it to their incentives and rewards.

Principle 3: Build a Trusting and Collaborative Culture

Ryan, a senior vice president at a technology company, was a rising star known for delivering results.

During his mid-year review, his COO shared feedback from Ryan's team of vice presidents. His style felt too directive, and his weekly meetings had become task-assignment sessions, not forums for ideas. Feeling undervalued and wary of challenging him, team members had stopped speaking up.

Ryan disagreed.

"I have more experience than my team. That's why I need to be the one making the decisions," he explained.

"No," the COO responded. "Your team collectively has far more experience than any one person." That response got Ryan's attention.

When he met with Cornelia for their first coaching session, he was unconvinced but unsettled.

"I'm an effective leader. If people had an issue, they would've told me," he shared. "My team needs a lot of pushing, and I'm doing most of the heavy lifting. We need to move fast to hit our targets."

Cornelia acknowledged his perspective and his past success. Then she asked, "Do you think there are other good approaches within your team that could help your division's performance? And if there are, why do you think people might be holding them back instead of sharing them with you?"

Ryan paused, considering whether there was a gap between his intentions and how his team experienced his leadership.

"I'm going to try a small experiment," Ryan said. "I'm going to make a point of inviting my team to share ideas at the next three meetings and then step back and just listen."

The first time he did, he only got a few cautious responses, but even those small comments revealed ideas and perspectives he hadn't heard before. Over the next few coaching sessions, Ryan realized his drive for efficiency was unintentionally discouraging his team from speaking up. Determined to rebuild trust, he began acknowledging every contribution, asking follow-up questions, and making a point to thank people for their input, whether or not it aligned with his own views.

Gradually, the atmosphere started shifting. As Ryan listened more and spoke less, tension gave way to constructive dialogue. Within six months, his reengaged vice presidents started sharing and implementing their own innovative ideas. For the first time since stepping into his role, Ryan no longer felt he was carrying the weight alone. The newly energized team cocreated a strategy that over the next year propelled their performance far beyond what they had originally imagined.

The lesson is clear: To unlock your team's panoramic leadership, you must create an environment of trust where people feel safe to share their ideas—even those that contradict your own.

Embed Panoramic Leadership into Your Schedule

The three principles we've just explored gain their real power when they're put into practice consistently. By making these principles a regular part of leadership, you build clarity, alignment, and open dialogue into the way your team works every day.

Recall that Alan Mulally made his Business Plan Review process a rigorous habit. In addition to the psychological safety he created in the meetings and the clear prioritizing done by the green, yellow, and red traffic light system, it was the clockwork regularity of the reviews that made them so effective. They were held every Thursday morning throughout Alan's tenure with Ford. Alan told his team the meetings weren't optional, and he reinforced their importance by showing up to nearly every one throughout his years of leadership at Boeing and later at Ford. He shared with us,

> I think I missed personally attending only twelve BPRs, in all my years at Boeing and Ford. And those I missed were because I was either on an airplane or I was somewhere with the kids. In that case, I would dial in or teleconference in, and the kids loved it. They could watch everybody changing their colors and clapping for each other—they just went berserk about that.[2]

This discipline became a cornerstone of Ford's transformation—achieved without a government bailout—and contributed to one of the most significant corporate turnarounds of the modern era.

So, in whatever way you implement panoramic leadership in your organization, get it on the schedule and emphatically impress upon people that participation is not optional and can't be delegated. Remember, achieving panoramic leadership doesn't have to take lots of time. The whole business plan review process for Alan's multibillion-dollar global companies took just a few hours to complete.

Taken together, the three principles—and the practice of making panoramic leadership a routine—will help you build the discipline and focus you need to stay aligned on priorities and deliver meaningful results. In the next chapter, we're going to look at how to make panoramic leadership a way of life. But before we turn to that, here are some questions that will help you work out how to apply the principles described in this chapter in your own working life.

QUESTIONS TO CONSIDER

- What are my team's top priorities, and how do I ensure they remain clear despite competing demands?
- When everything seems urgent, how do I avoid just "putting out fires" and instead focus on what truly matters for the long-term goals?
- Is my personal incentive plan (the way I reward or discipline myself) aligned with my deeply held values and the long-term vision of my work?
- How can I create a safe culture within my own mind—one that allows insights from different stakeholders to question my assumptions without triggering defensiveness?
- What steps can I take to build a culture of openness and trust in my organization, where people feel comfortable sharing differing opinions or negative feedback without fear of being dismissed?
- How do I make panoramic leadership a routine in my organization?

PART THREE

CULTIVATING PERSONAL GROWTH AND EMPOWERING OTHERS

CHAPTER 9

A Way of Life

Now that you understand the power of panoramic leadership and have the tools you need to achieve it, there's one more thing we want you to know. Practicing panoramic leadership is not a one-and-done event, rolled out only for special occasions or filed away and quickly forgotten. Instead, it's a lifelong practice that can bring you and those around you more success, fulfillment, and joy. This can happen not just in your career and work but in your personal life as well.

In this chapter, we show you how.

To begin, we'd like to introduce you to Parth Patil, a digital pioneer who builds AI agents, conversational interfaces, and intelligent software. In addition, he currently works for LinkedIn cofounder Reid Hoffman as his personal expert on AI.

After graduating from UCLA in 2017, Parth worked in a variety of jobs, eventually landing the position of data scientist for the Clubhouse social audio app. While he was at Clubhouse, he sensed something really big was on the horizon in computing. That something turned out to be GPT, OpenAI's large language model and the technology that powers ChatGPT.

As Parth tells us,

> I met so many people on Clubhouse, and GPT was the most popular topic on the app at the time. Everyone was talking about GPT—all around the world. I was asking people, "How are you using this?" Then I met farmers in India who were using it for crop-cycle planning, and that's when I had my epiphany—this is for all intents and purposes a new computer.[1]

One of Parth's friends on the Clubhouse app—whom he had never met in person—was programming with GPT. After this friend got access to GPT-4, he urged Parth, "This thing is really smart. You should have *it* teach you programming." Some of Parth's smartest engineering friends had even left their jobs to go work for OpenAI.

With his curiosity ignited, Parth decided to dive in deeper. He watched a YouTube video that showed that if you tell GPT about a type of program you want it to write, speaking in plain English, it'll immediately launch into writing that program for you.

He decided to build his first software agent using GPT-4 in his free time. After work, he devoted the rest of his day to this project, using the agent to generate a hundred prototypes, each one based on a unique idea. He wanted to see the full panorama of what was possible. Then he created a second agent and told it, "Take this list of a hundred ideas and make the first version of everything." Parth, meanwhile, went for a nap. When he came back after several hours, his software agent had created a hundred prototypes.

While only around 30 percent of those prototypes worked, Parth knew he was onto something that could change the world as he knew it. "It was like magic," he tells us. "The whole point of computers is for them to do what you want them to. And now you can just say to the computer, 'Go do this thing.'"

What really shocked Parth was when he realized that GPT could do his job better than he could. "I woke up in the middle of the night, and I had an anxiety attack. I was thinking, *What am I doing? This GPT is a better data scientist than me.* This is the thing I thought I was good at—the thing I dedicated my career to." But he didn't let his ego get in the way. Driven by optimistic fear, he got up close to this new technology and started seeing new perspectives.

April 2023 was a brutal time for tech companies, and Parth was laid off from his position at Clubhouse. However, instead of looking for a new job, he devoted himself entirely to experimenting in this new world of AI agents. He was able to support himself by burning through his severance and then his 401(k) retirement savings. "I would just sit there at my desk, talk to GPT4, and program every single day. I was thinking, *Okay, if you don't have a job, you might as well work Saturday and Sunday too—you're not going to be doing this forever*. I'm okay having zero dollars to my name if I know where the future is going." The future, he was sure, would value knowledge of AI.

For the first few months, Parth's friends thought he was going through some sort of personal crisis. Why would he decide to forgo employment to explore this new world? "You're crazy," they would tell him. However, they eventually began to see that Parth was doing some amazing things with his AI agents. Word about what he was up to got around, and one day a company CFO invited Parth to lunch and said to him, "I'll pay you to teach me how to think like you."

Parth couldn't believe it. *What?* he thought to himself. *Someone will pay me to show them how I think?* Indeed, they would. This CFO had understood the power of Parth's perspective and wanted to incorporate part of Parth's map into his own. "We would sit together every week," Parth continues, "and program for four hours until his mind felt completely saturated with information. But then he'd come back the next week, and we'd program some more." Parth took on a few more clients doing the same thing and also did an occasional consulting job implementing large language models.

One of Parth's teammates on a project, Ben, was working with LinkedIn cofounder Reid Hoffman, and he asked Parth if he could build a custom GPT that could draw from Reid's vast body of work, such as his books, podcasts, and LinkedIn posts. "I already knew how to do that," explained Parth. "That was one of the many architectures of GPT that I'd been thinking about." And within two and a half hours, Parth sent the first version to Ben. "His mind was blown by how fast I did it," Parth says. Ben suggested he should come to the Bay Area and meet Reid.

When Reid asked Parth, "How long are you here?" Parth replied, "I haven't booked my flight back."

"Come back tomorrow, Parth," Reid responded. "We'll go deep on this."

When Parth met Reid the next day, they talked for four and a half hours. "I want to understand how you think about agents, what you think about the future," Reid told Parth. And Parth shared his map, telling Reid about all the projects he was exploring, the realizations he'd had, and what he felt the implications were.

The next day, Reid asked his team to make Parth an offer. He accepted, and he's carried on exploring ever since.

By following the lead of his curiosity and having the courage to forego making an income for months, Parth gathered the panoramic intelligence to reach out to new learning and transform his life. In the process, by connecting new dots in his career, he dramatically reshaped its trajectory.

You, too, can use panoramic leadership practices to consider new possibilities for your life, modifying your course or perhaps setting an altogether new one.

In the pages that follow, we introduce a handful of additional practices you can adopt right now to widen your perspective and improve your personal life and the lives of those around you. Your family, friends, neighbors, the community in which you live, and even people far beyond can all benefit when you turn these practices into lifelong habits.

Marshall's Life Plan Review

More efficiently and more effectively than most any other technique we're aware of, the business plan review process Alan Mulally developed can help you close the gap between what you plan to do in your business and what you actually get done.

But what if you could find a way to close the gap between what you plan to do and what you actually get done in your *life*? That's where Marshall's idea of a life plan review (LPR) comes in. Marshall based his LPR process both on Alan's business plan review and on his own many years of coaching. When you adopt the life plan review and make it a weekly habit, you'll move forward in life by being more accountable for your behavior and your goals.

In his book, *The Earned Life*, Marshall explains that the method you use to conduct a life plan review is contained in those three words: Life. Plan. Review. You first decide what you want your *life* to be and what the future looks like if everything goes according to *plan*. You then conduct a weekly *review* of your effort to earn the life that you want.

This approach is unique because it doesn't rely on your becoming more heroic in motivation, habit, resourcefulness, or courage. It assumes that you're *human,* which means you're going to fall short of perfection. So it asks only that you pay attention to your level of effort.

The process comprises three steps.

Step 1: Engage in weekly meetings where you answer fixed questions with a partner to improve your life. Instead of reporting your results, you grade your *effort* on a 1-to-10 scale, with 1 being lowest and 10 being highest. Here are six questions Marshall suggests you and your partner ask each other, though you are welcome to come up with your own. Each begins with "Did I do my best to . . .":

- Set clear goals?
- Make progress toward achieving my goals?
- Find meaning?
- Be happy?
- Maintain and build positive relationships?
- Be fully engaged?

The real power of the LPR process comes from involving someone else in it. Sure, you can go through the motions of the LPR process all by yourself, but you won't get the benefit of being answerable to other people on a regular basis. In addition, when you involve someone else, you overcome one of the biggest obstacles many of us face in our day-to-day lives: asking for help.

Step 2: Self-monitor between weekly meetings, asking yourself the six questions every day. While it's not important what time of the day you do this, Marshall likes to score himself at the end of each day. The most important thing is to make it a habit. Every day. Without fail.

Step 3: Review your plan once a week to ensure it is still relevant. As time goes on, your goals typically change, and it makes sense to put less effort into ones you're no longer interested in. Or perhaps you've achieved them! So, if you notice that you're putting less effort into certain goals, consider whether you've outgrown them, and think about new ones that are more relevant to where you are today.

Answering these questions has brought Cornelia great comfort. Looking back through her answers over time, she's seen that she's made progress nearly every day toward her goals. This has helped her keep in mind that we shouldn't just focus on the end goal but also on our daily progress—and to savor the journey. Otherwise, we miss many opportunities to recognize our progress along the way. We need to take time to celebrate steps one to ninety-nine and not just step one hundred.

Alan Mulally's Family Plan Review

We all want to improve and get better at what we do, whatever it may be, and if you want to improve at something, you need to measure your progress. However, while most of us are used to measuring things at work—new customers your sales team acquired, the number of visitors your website attracted last month, how much your revenue increased—few of us measure what we do at home.

Alan Mulally realized that the same process that drives high-performing teams at work can also strengthen trust, accountability, and connection at home. His insight became the foundation for what he called the "Family Plan Review."

While he was studying engineering at the University of Kansas, Alan met Nicki, his future wife. The happy couple was married in 1970. As Alan told us, "Nicki and I both came from large families, and we decided that we were going to have five children." Keeping up with all five kids was proving a challenge, and, as Alan recalls, "One day I came home from work, and I told Nicki I thought we needed to have a business plan review every week with our family."

To Alan's surprise, Nicki didn't exactly jump at the opportunity. "Alan, this is not Boeing," she replied. She knew all about the review process, and she was decidedly uninterested.

So Alan rethought his idea and tried again. "I came back the next week, and I said, 'Okay, Nicki, I really think we ought to have a *family* plan review every week.'"

"Really?" she asked Alan. "What would the agenda be like?"

"The first thing would be," Alan responded, "after we come home from church on Sunday, for each one of us—including you and me—to go around the house, pick up all our stuff, and take it back to our rooms or our cubbies. The house looks like a bomb's gone off, with stuff all over the place."

"That's a great idea," Nicki agreed. "And the fact that we're all doing it together, with us showing our kids what it looks like to do it, that sounds great. What's the next agenda item?"

Alan was starting to convince her.

"After that, everybody will go back to their bedrooms, including you and me separately, and we'll pick up our clothes and we'll bring them down to the laundry, and we can do all of it once a week, on Sundays." (Now, mind you, they had an advantage in doing all the laundry at once; they had two washers and two dryers.) That would take a big burden off of Nicki, who'd been doing the laundry. "No one signs up for a life where you do everyone's laundry every week," Alan said.

Nicki loved the idea.

"And when the laundry's done," Alan continued, "we'll lay it all out on the kitchen table and then we'll work together to sort the socks and everything else. So we'll be down to two minutes, and it'll be all sorted for seven people. And we won't have to memorize everybody's items."

"What's next?" asked Nicki.

"Everyone will go back to their rooms to get their calendars and notebooks to take notes." Alan continued, "We'll go around the table, and everybody'll describe what they're going to do the next week and what help they need. So, if they need taxicab service, they'll say that, and we can all help. Then they'll write this down."

As Alan explains, "We had a version of our family's Working Together principles and practices, and we'd go through it in the meeting. Then, if anyone had a question about them, or if they had an experience where someone didn't follow the principles and practices, the idea was to share it in front of all of us so we could learn from it."

One time, for example, their daughter Molly had a dance recital coming up. Alan recalls, "She said during the Sunday meeting, 'I need somebody to help me with a ride to my recital this week, if that would work for you guys.'" Her older brother Chris had just gotten his driver's license and said he'd be happy to take her.

"Great!" Molly said, writing it down on her calendar as Chris wrote it down on his.

Alan continues, "The next week we had our family meeting, and we got to Molly's recital. She said, 'I have something I would like to share. Chris, I know that you just must have forgotten that you were going to pick me up, and I didn't get a chance to go to my recital.' Those words got her brother's attention right away. Then Molly continued, 'I just wanted you to know that the reason that I was so happy you were going to take me was not for the drive, but I wanted to introduce you to everybody there because you're a great older brother. You're in high school, you're an athlete, and I think you're great. I also wanted to share with you what I've learned from all my dancing.'"

"We were all looking at Chris," says Alan, "and his face was as pale as it could be—all the color had drained right out of it. Think about what that kind of conversation with the family meant to everybody. Everybody had learned through our family meetings how to love each other up, including how to share with them when they had an issue."

While Alan says that his kids will admit today that they didn't always enjoy the weekly family meetings—they could be tough—they made a point to never miss one. And that's no surprise when you learn what the last item on the agenda was. That's when Alan handed out the kids' allowances.[2]

The Power of Keeping a Journal

Each day of our lives is filled with countless events, interactions, and emotions, often blending into one big chaotic jumble. If you're not already doing so, we have a simple suggestion for you: Keep a journal.

We recommend journaling daily. The time of day doesn't matter, nor does it matter how you choose to do it, whether with a pen and paper, a spiral notebook, or using a journaling app. What's important is that you make it a regular practice. For example, when you take a break at lunch, at the end of the day, or on a train commute home, check in with yourself and write down any strong emotions you felt. What made you happy, sad, or angry? What accomplishments from the day are you proudest of? Are you feeling nervous, anxious, or worried? Why?

Even for a minute each day, journaling offers a variety of benefits beyond just documenting your life. It creates mental clarity, helping you see through the fog by organizing your thoughts, spotting patterns, and making connections that might otherwise remain hidden. It gives you a safe, private space to express your true feelings, easing stress and anxiety over recent events and enhancing self-awareness.

In this world of constant change, we need to tune in carefully to our emotions. A main problem that journaling helps us solve is that many of us are not as in touch with our emotions as we could be. We need to figure out what triggers us to feel good and bad, which can be difficult to perceive. Because we can misinterpret what we're feeling, the first step is for you to name the emotion you're actually experiencing. You might be sad yet initially label it as anger—especially as social norms may discourage expressing sadness. The more attuned you are to the specific emotions you're feeling, the easier it'll be to figure out why you're feeling them.

Journaling is more than just reflection. It also offers a lens to reinterpret your experiences and reshape your narrative to yourself. One powerful illustration of this comes from a story shared by storyteller Donald Davis.

In his TEDx Talk, Donald recounts the story of his father, Joe, who at five years old accidentally cut himself in the leg with an ax. Joe's father loaded him onto a horse, and after refusing to allow his son's leg to be amputated by the country doctor, took him on a 172-mile train ride to Atlanta. There, Joe's leg was treated by a doctor who removed the kneecap, leaving a leg that would barely bend and a very large indent.[3]

Joe's mother was concerned about how this incident would affect his life, and she told him he should tell the story of the incident over and over again—each time from the perspective of a different person involved. She suggested he begin with his own perspective and what he learned by living through the experience, then his parents' perspective, and then the perspective of his doctor in Atlanta, and so on.

She explained that when something painful happens, it can feel like a heavy rock sitting on top of you. If you don't tell the story enough, that weight stays with you. But when you begin to talk about it and share the story, you start to lift the weight off until it becomes something you can sit on top of rather than something that holds you down.[4]

Joe followed his mother's sage advice and ended up telling the story over and over—he reckoned at least two hundred times—taking a panoramic view of the story from the perspective of many stakeholders involved. Through the mix of these panoramic perspectives, Joe gained a deeper understanding of how different people played a part in the story and how others saw him.

Most importantly, he defined his own feelings about the incident and his relationship with what he lived through. This helped him process his emotions until one day he decided that the benefits of his injury were wonderful. Joe realized he didn't have to work on the farm. He made the shift to a career in banking, which put him in a much better position to support his family.

Similarly, your *relationship* to the events that happened during your day is just as important as the events themselves. This relationship will determine what you do in the future with everything related to the events, the people involved in them, and anything that reminds you of the events. And yes, keeping a journal is a terrific way to understand this relationship and widen your perspective and panoramic vision.

Cornelia keeps a journal every day to gain a more panoramic view of what makes her happy in her life, what makes her sad or stressed, and how to move toward a greater level of fulfillment. In this journal, Cornelia starts with her own perspective—how she's feeling, what made her happy during the day, and what didn't. Then she broadens her view, considering the perspectives of key people involved in these events, and replaying the scenario from their points of view. This helps her better understand her own relationship to events that made her feel happy, sad, or frustrated. She often ends with a feeling of gratitude to the people involved, and sometimes with a note to follow up with them.

Finally, journaling helps you get past the nearsightedness of immediate gratification and to see over the horizon to your longer-term goals. It helps you gain distance from your day-to-day tasks, enabling you to see farther and regularly consider how you're progressing toward where you truly want to be.

Robert Waldinger and Happiness

Panoramic leadership highlights one of the most important ways to find happiness and fulfillment—the power of human connection. Growing meaningful relationships with stakeholders goes a long way in building productive channels of communication and creating opportunities to spark positive social connections.

One of the leading voices on the study of well-being is Dr. Robert Waldinger, who has devoted much of his career to understanding what makes life fulfilling. A psychiatrist, ordained Zen Buddhist teacher, and director of the Harvard Study on Adult Development, he oversees the longest-running study on the biological processes and psychosocial variables in early life that predict health and well-being in late life.

While the study revealed all sorts of data about the people who participated in it—including health outcomes and participants' success in relationships and careers, or the lack thereof—the basic hope when the study was initiated in 1938 was that it would provide hints on what it took to lead a healthy and happy life. It provided more than hints.

The study produced solid evidence about one of the most important sources of both happiness and good health, revealing a strong link between how satisfied people are in their relationships and their level of physical health as they get older. In his popular TED Talk, "What Makes a Good Life?" Waldinger says about the study participants, "When we gathered together everything we knew about them about at age fifty, it wasn't their middle-age cholesterol levels that predicted how they were going to grow old, it was how satisfied they were in their relationships. The people who were the most satisfied in their relationships at age fifty were the healthiest at age eighty."[5]

According to Waldinger, the main message from this study is remarkably simple but incredibly powerful: "Good relationships keep us happier and healthier."

Tragically, many people lack strong relationships. It's no secret that there's an epidemic of loneliness today. When a recent study asked US adults how close they felt to others emotionally, just 39 percent of them responded that they felt very connected to others.[6]

No one can go it alone, and it's more fulfilling to create and nurture relationships—especially with a full panorama of stakeholders, from our friends and families, to colleagues and coworkers, to neighbors and partners in our communities.

In their book *The Good Life*, Waldinger and Marc Schulz suggest that we plot our social universe—everyone with whom we have a relationship—on a chart to determine how energizing and how depleting our relationships are, along with the frequency of our interactions.

They distinguish between relationships that energize us and those that deplete us. Energizing relationships generally leave us feeling more alive, more connected, and strengthened. Depleting relationships do the opposite—they create tension or anxiety and leave us feeling more isolated than we would have felt on our own.

To get started with the plot of your social universe, Waldinger and Schulz suggest that you make a list of the key people in your life. Then choose one and put that person on your plot. Does this person uplift you or drain you? Do you see them infrequently or frequently?

Next, if you'd like to change where that person is on your plot, draw an arrow to the spot where you'd like them to be. Then consider how to achieve this. Maybe a relationship with a friend has become draining, and you realize that this is because you're not spending enough time together. You're feeling sad about the relationship because you feel you're losing touch. Draw an arrow to a more uplifting spot on your plot and commit to suggesting that you and this friend meet up more often.

Your Relationship Energy Plan

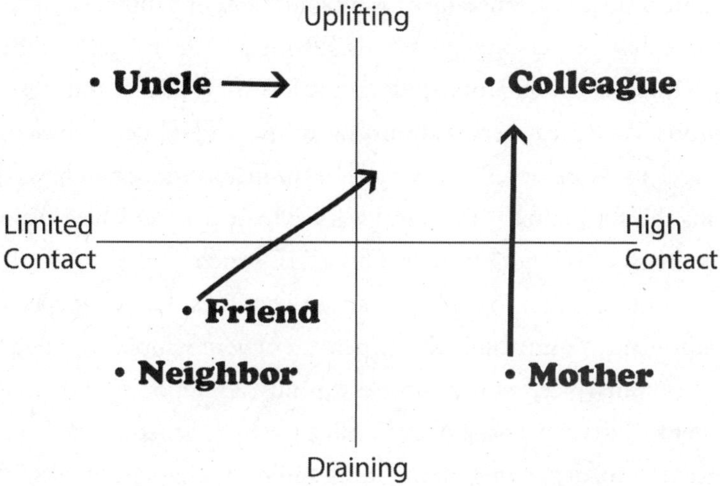

Based on concepts from Robert Waldinger and Marc Schulz, *The Good Life: Lessons from the World's Longest Scientific Study of Happiness* (Simon & Schuster, 2023).

As a practice in panoramic leadership, this exercise isn't about labeling relationships as good or bad. It's about noticing what they're telling us. When we step back and look at our relationships as a whole, our field of view widens. We start to see patterns we might miss when we're caught up in day-to-day interactions. A relationship that feels depleting, for example, may not be a signal to walk away, but rather a clue. Something important may need attention, repair, or simply more presence. According to the authors, "In truth, almost all relationships contain opportunities; we just have to identify them."[7]

Panoramic leaders learn to pay attention to these signals, understanding that the relationships they nurture quietly shape both the decisions they make and the lives they lead.

Happiness Hoarding

Arthur Brooks has done a lot of work in the area of happiness. In fact, he says that his personal mission is "lifting people up and bringing them together in bonds of happiness and love using science and ideas."[8] Sounds like a great personal mission to us. And while he does this research to lift up other people, he'll be the first to admit that he's also doing this for himself. "Frankly, I wanted to be happier," he explains. "You know, this is not research. This is ME-search."[9]

Brooks goes on to explain that our happiness has three specific components. "Something like 25 percent of your happiness is due to your circumstance," which, Brooks explains, is temporary and impermanent. "Fifty percent of your baseline levels are genetic. The last 25 percent or so, depending on the study you're looking at, is habits."[10]

Happiness can give us boosts of energy. To get such boosts, we can notice small things that cheer us up—a favorite song coming on the radio, a pleasant memory that makes us smile, or a coworker who compliments us. We should tune our minds to paying attention to these little events in our lives, allowing them to uplift us.

One obstacle to us doing this is what Cornelia calls *happiness hoarding*—behaviors designed to accumulate happiness by limiting others' experiences of joy. Examples are:

- **Hoarding a feeling of control.** You overly restrict or micromanage others, denying them autonomy, or demanding that everything be done your way because you've "thought it through."
- **Hoarding the feeling of accomplishment.** You take all the credit for coming up with an idea or a new initiative at work, neglecting to share credit with other contributors.

- **Hoarding a feeling of power.** You actively undermine someone else's authority or influence in order to gain an advantage or reinforce your superiority.
- **Hoarding a feeling of bonding.** When you become highly inclusive with some people, you can intentionally or inadvertently lead others to feel excluded, such as when you meet exclusively with a certain group and neglect to acknowledge others in the room outside of this group.

The more tightly we try to hold on to joy, though, the faster it slips through our grasp. Happiness, like perspective, is inherently panoramic: It expands when shared. When leaders cling to it, they isolate; when they circulate it, they connect. Over time, happiness hoarding can narrow our vision and make our maps less expansive and informative. Panoramic leaders learn to release that grasp, allowing joy to flow through teams and relationships. In doing so, they rediscover an essential truth of leadership and life: fulfillment is not something we keep but something we create together, in motion.

In the end, cultivating happiness and nurturing our emotional well-being are not passive pursuits but intentional practices that shape the quality of our relationships and lives. By appreciating positive moments, fostering genuine connection, and consciously sharing the rewards of happiness with those around us, we enrich our own lives while also helping to create a more enjoyable and vibrant world. Let's remember that the small choices we make can set in motion waves of positivity that extend far beyond ourselves.

The Gift of Gratitude

A wealth of research has found that expressing gratitude toward others enhances our lives in many ways. According to a Harvard Health Publishing article, expressing gratitude has the power to make you more optimistic and feel better about your life, increase your happiness, manage adversity, strengthen relationships, and enhance your health.[11] It also inspires those who receive it. When you express gratitude to others, you're widening their view of the positive impacts they have in the world around them—the good they do.

Chester Elton is a good friend and colleague of ours. In addition to being a member of Marshall's 100 Coaches Program, he's a *New York Times* bestselling author, a Thinkers50 executive coach, and a culture and leadership expert. When it comes to making panoramic leadership a lifelong practice, there's one thing in particular about Chester we'd like to highlight: his focus on the power of gratitude.

In his book *Leading with Gratitude*, coauthored with Adrian Gostick, Chester explains that showing gratitude to employees is the easiest, fastest, and most inexpensive way to improve performance. The authors emphasize expressing gratitude to our peers at work, which fits perfectly with our own experience sharing perspectives with peers. Chester and Adrian write, "When employees are grateful to each other, they affirm positive, vital concepts typically valued in their colleagues such as trustworthiness, dependability, and talent. Peer-to-peer gratitude is particularly powerful because it comes from people who are greatly respected—their fellow team members. And this can have an invigorating effect on organizations overall."[12]

Expressing gratitude is a great way to maintain relationships with our stakeholders, just as Alan Mulally and Ford's executives shared their love with the company's dealers on Ford Field.

As we practice expressing gratitude to others, it's important that we also regularly express gratitude to ourselves. Emma Seppälä, science director of the Center for Compassion and Altruism Research and Education at Stanford University and codirector of the Yale College Emotional Intelligence Project, emphasizes this. "When we take note of our positive qualities and are grateful for them, we become more self-compassionate—not to mention that we start to see ourselves in a much more realistic and positive light."[13] Even if you also see real weaknesses in yourself, addressing them from a place of self-compassion will help you thrive.

Gratitude is a recognition of connection—the quiet acknowledgment that none of us leads or grows alone. As Guy Kawasaki reminds us, "Express your gratitude to those who've helped you along the way. You never know when a simple 'thank you' might make all the difference in someone's life. And you never know when a person's time is up, and you won't get to express your gratitude."[14]

The key is to make expressing gratitude a lifelong practice and not just a one-and-done thing. Motivational speaker Zig Ziglar once said, "Gratitude is the healthiest of all human emotions. The more you express gratitude for what you have, the more likely you will have even more to express gratitude for."

Interconnectedness, Impermanence, and Acceptance: A Buddhist Perspective

You may not know that Marshall has been a philosophical Buddhist for decades. What he loves about Buddhism is that the tenets can be applied by anyone, no matter what their beliefs are or aren't. And Marshall says that his Buddhist philosophy has helped cure him of the great Western disease of saying or thinking, "I'll be happy when . . ." followed by something like, "I buy a shiny, new car," or "We've got $1 million set aside for retirement," or "We're able to afford a monthlong cruise ship vacation."

The thing is, when we finally achieve whatever that goal is, we're never really happy. The goalposts move farther out, always just out of our reach. In thinking this way, we're also making the mistake of fixating on the future instead of enjoying the life we're living right now. Bob Waldinger and Marc Schulz discuss this concept in *The Good Life*:

> We are resilient, industrious, and creative creatures who can survive incredible hardship, laugh our way through tough times, and come out stronger on the other end. But there's another side to this, as the concept of a happiness set point and research about lottery winners shows: We also get used to *better* circumstances. Our emotional well-being cannot improve into infinity. We settle in. We tend to take things for granted. This is a key point in the discussion about money. You might believe that making six figures or landing a new job or upgrading from your old Honda will make you happy, but in short order you will have gotten used to that situation, too, and your brain will move on to the next challenge, the next desire. Not even lottery winners can remain euphoric forever.
>
> This does not point to a flaw in the human character, but to a biological fact: We meet all experiences, positive and negative, on the same psychological and neurological playing field in our brain. Here the science dovetails with a central tenet of Stoicism and Buddhism, as well as many other spiritual traditions: The way we feel in life is determined only in part by what happens around us, and to a great extent by what happens inside of us.[15]

Three keys to Buddhist thought are the concepts of interconnectedness, impermanence, and acceptance, which are deeply intertwined.

Interconnectedness means nothing exists independently. Because everything arises within a web of shifting causes and conditions, nothing is permanently separate or fixed. We only exist in relation to everything else.

Impermanence is realizing that everything is constantly changing, so nothing lasts forever. The success we enjoy today may be gone tomorrow. The sorrow we suffer today will fade in time. Everything in this world is subject to change.

Acceptance is making peace with impermanence and living your life accordingly. That means enjoying the life we're living now instead of being fixated on a "better" future that in reality exists only in our minds. When you accept the impermanence of life, you'll be better able to focus on the rich panorama of opportunities for joy and meaning that surround you.

Marshall tells the story about the time he was on a flight from Zurich to New York, and he sat next to a wealthy investor. The investor was upset because he'd discovered he paid too much for a small high-tech company, and he was mad at the founder for misleading him. Revenue targets were missed, and the founder turned out to be an unmotivated slacker who couldn't seem to keep any business commitments. And there the investor sat, in his first-class seat, beating himself up about the acquisition.

To an objective observer, the investor had a great life. He had made many successful investments in companies and had millions in the bank, a gorgeous home, and a loving family. By all rights, he should have been a very happy guy, but he was miserable.

Marshall suggested to him that maybe he wasn't as angry at the founder as he was at himself for being a poor judge of character and not conducting adequate due diligence in the purchase. The investor agreed that might be the case, and then remained focused on his mistake. "I usually have a great instinct for these deals. How did I screw this one up?"

Marshall reminded the investor that despite this one mistake, he was still very successful. He suggested the investor write off this bad deal as an experience he could learn from and apply to his next acquisition. But to stop beating himself up, Marshall explained, the investor had to go farther than that. He had to accept the situation, and he also had to forgive both of the people involved.

"Let me ask you something," Marshall said to the investor. "How much sleep do you think this person is losing over you right now?"

"None."

"So, who is being punished here? And who is doing the punishing?" Marshall asked.

The response from the investor was immediate: "That would be me—twice." He began to see how refusing to accept the situation he had created led him to torture himself about it.

"What do you suggest?" he asked Marshall.

"Well," replied Marshall, "I'd either fire the founder or sell the company. But before that, I'd work on forgiving myself." Accepting the situation and realizing that he doesn't need to dwell on his failure forever would help the investor forgive himself. The investor's misery was part of a complex web of interconnected causes, both internal and external. His anger at the founder for misleading him was closely linked to his deeper anger at himself and resulted in his self-punishment. Understanding this interconnectedness can lead to compassion, initially for oneself and then for others, moving away from self-torture and toward a path of healing and potential well-being.

Accepting life's impermanence can free you to see more opportunities in your life. The perspective of the investor sitting next to Marshall on that flight to New York was so narrowly focused on one deal gone wrong that he was stuck. He couldn't see the full panorama of all the good things he had in his life. He could only see that narrow sliver of pessimistic fear within himself, and this made him so afraid of making the same mistake again that he ignored the opportunity to learn and grow and continue on to further success.

Embrace impermanence, interconnectedness, and acceptance in your own life. You'll see a much richer landscape around you—sure, sometimes the bad things, but especially, and much more often, opportunities for the good things.

Now that we've explored making panoramic leadership a way of life, in the next and final chapter, we show how you can help others become panoramic leaders. We do this through the stories of a number of exceptional leaders who passionately devoted themselves to expanding others' horizons. But before turning to those stories, here are some questions for you to consider that can help you make the concepts of panoramic leadership part of your everyday life and become happier in the process.

QUESTIONS TO CONSIDER

- What daily practices help me reflect on what brings me happiness, sadness, or stress?
- What deeper understanding might I gain by telling an important story in my life from multiple viewpoints—my own and those of others involved? How could this help me process my emotions and redefine how I feel about the situation?

- In what areas of my nonprofessional life could I follow my courageous curiosity and dive deeper into new possibilities, even if it requires a period of immediate discomfort?
- Reflecting on Dr. Robert Waldinger's research, how satisfied am I with my current relationships, and what specific actions can I take to cultivate good relationships that keep me happier and healthier?
- How can I make gratitude a more consistent part of my daily interactions with colleagues, friends, family, and myself? How might practicing gratitude strengthen my well-being and relationships?
- In what ways do I find myself saying, "I'll be happy when . . ."? How can embracing the concepts of interconnectedness, impermanence, and acceptance help me find joy and meaning in the present moment?

CHAPTER 10

Help Others Become Panoramic Leaders

We can't forget that an important part of being a panoramic leader is to lead others. Marshall often quotes one of his clients: "While achievement may be 'all about me,' leadership is 'all about them.'"

Becoming a panoramic leader has the power to bring more success and happiness to you in your business and personal life. But we believe that's just the first step. The next step is for you to help others find the same success and happiness you've achieved by teaching them how to become panoramic leaders. By taking this next step, you'll make an even bigger contribution to the world.

You might remember a time when you were a child and you threw a rock in a river or pool of water and were fascinated by the circles that rippled out from the point of impact. Similarly, our actions ripple out from our personal point of impact, affecting the people around us.

Nothing we do happens in isolation. Everything we do, no matter how small, has consequences, positive or negative, and our actions often affect people we don't even know far into the future. In the words of Zen Buddhist master Thich Nhat Hanh, "My actions are my only true belongings. I cannot escape the consequences of my actions. My actions are the ground on which I stand."[1]

Our challenge to you in this final chapter is to look outside yourself and consider how you can teach others the lessons you've learned in this book. When you do that, the ripples you create will extend far out from you, having a positive impact on people you know—and people you don't know.

In the pages that follow, we share stories of how a number of influential panoramic leaders have helped others develop these skills, multiplying their impact far beyond themselves for years to come.

How Indra Nooyi's Leadership Rippled Across PepsiCo's Stakeholders

Indra Nooyi served as chairman and CEO of PepsiCo for just over twelve years, and during that time the company's net revenue increased by more than 80 percent.[2] Equally as impressive as those results is how she reached out to PepsiCo's many stakeholders to transform the business while also raising awareness across the food industry—and beyond—about the need for healthier food.

In 2006, Indra laid out a new mission, her Performance with Purpose (PwP) initiative, a framework that recognized that PepsiCo's long-term financial success required more than creating value for shareholders; it required creating value for multiple additional stakeholders, including customers, employees, suppliers, and communities in which the company operated.

Key to PwP was her concern that PepsiCo's products contained too much sugar, fat, and salt. Health advocates had spotlighted that these ingredients could contribute to all sorts of health problems, including diabetes, obesity, and hypertension.

Indra perceived the seriousness of the problem, and the input she received from others about the issue increased her determination to address it. She recounts in her book *My Life in Full*,

> I was once in Egypt having dinner with our local leaders and their spouses, and one of the women told me how she was reluctant to let her children consume our products because they lacked nutritional value. This was incredibly honest—and useful for me. That someone could be so blunt, even when her family's income counted on PepsiCo, amped up my sense of urgency to do something about it.[3]

Indra was convinced that if PepsiCo were to continue to succeed, the company would have to change. As Daniel Pink observes, "The most deeply motivated people—not to mention those who are most productive and satisfied—hitch their desires to a cause larger than themselves."[4] That's exactly what Indra did: She reimagined PepsiCo's mission to serve not only shareholders but also employees, customers, and communities, linking business performance to human and environmental well-being.

But making the kind of major pivot required is easier said than done for successful companies, especially successful *large* companies, because many leaders within, from middle managers to executives, often resist. As Indra wrote in a *Harvard Business Review* article, "At companies that have performed well, sometimes for decades, it's natural for employees to continue the behaviors that have led to strong results. Success, more than failure, prevents a company's transformation."[5]

She recounts that some leaders at the company questioned why she launched PwP, with some pushing back hard. After an executive she hired made some comments about how the company had to change the way it marketed soft drinks to children to help combat obesity, "one company veteran went as far as to accuse the newcomer of being a saboteur and a traitor."[6]

Ultimately, succeeding with the PwP transformation required Indra to influence her employees, executives, the board, shareholders, and the industry as a whole to widen their perspectives and think more panoramically. She did this through an extensive series of meetings, presentations, speeches, interviews, media appearances, and industry forums. She recalls a speech she gave to four hundred of PepsiCo's top managers:

> If we didn't transform our portfolio to meet changing consumers, we couldn't grow . . . And if we didn't deliver performance, we couldn't fund purpose. Performance and purpose reinforced each other. It was a virtuous circle. I threw my head and heart into this speech . . . And, when I finished, the group stood up and cheered. I was relieved and ready to take it on the road.[7]

One group of stakeholders who posed a particular challenge was shareholders—especially some investors. "Shareholders wouldn't stand for anything that might affect PepsiCo's short-term profitability targets," she recalls. But Indra got up close to important investors to listen to their concerns and share her perspective. When activist investor Ralph Whitworth, who had bought $600 million of PepsiCo shares, questioned her strategy, she met with him and recounts, "I explained the strategy in detail. Ralph was smart and friendly, and, after a couple of discussions, he endorsed our plan. He told me to keep going; he did not want to waste any more of my time."[8]

Under Indra's leadership, PepsiCo made it a point to expand its offerings of more nutritious snacks and drinks. She hired a chief scientific officer to lead the development of recipes that were lower in sugar, salt, and fat, and the company acquired a number of healthier food brands, giving them much wider distribution.

Her efforts reached far beyond PepsiCo's own business. She urged top executives in the food and beverage industry to see more panoramically. In a speech she gave at a large industry conference about the necessity of creating healthier products, she shared, "Let's be a good industry that does what it possibly can—not grudgingly, but willingly, not as a last resort but as a first."[9] Around that time, a foundation was launched focusing on reducing obesity with the partnership of a wide variety of industry players. As Indra shared, "I took the bold step of addressing the industry association and saying, it's not one company that has to do something. All of us together have to act in unison to improve the food supply. And so we committed to the Healthy Weight Commitment Foundation."[10]

A set goal was to take out one and a half trillion calories from the US food system. "In reality," she continued, "we took almost six trillion calories out of the US food system, in a matter of about four years. And so I think that industry working together with a very clear idea of where we need to go can actually make a huge difference."[11] A 2014 study found that consumer packaged goods brands that joined the Healthy Weight Commitment Foundation pledge reduced calories sold by an average of seventy-eight calories per person per day—more than seven times the reduction seen in brands that did not participate.[12]

Since stepping down as CEO in 2018, the positive ripple effects of her efforts have continued to spread worldwide through the people she inspired to see more panoramically—encouraging others to lead with both vision and responsibility.

How Alan Mulally Inspired Panoramic Leadership Among Dealers

Earlier in this book, we shared the story of Alan Mulally's gathering of four thousand Ford dealership owners at Ford Field in Detroit, and we introduced you to one of those dealers, Dave Wilson. At the time of the gathering, in 2006, he was extremely concerned about the future of the company, which would be posting an enormous loss that year.[13]

Dave's concern turned to optimism as he listened to Alan that day—he became one of Alan's biggest fans. Alan encouraged the dealers, bonded with them, and understood them. Seeing this panoramic leadership in action, Dave adopted Alan's management philosophy and operating style, instituting his own business plan reviews to monitor progress and share perspectives on challenges. He recalls, "When I returned home from Detroit after hearing Alan speak for the first time, I remember telling our team that being a Ford dealer was going to be fun again. From that day forward I became a student of Alan Mulally, paying close attention to every move he made and how he conducted himself."[14]

Never doubt that you can create ripples of great leadership by showing others how to get up close, listen intently, and expand their maps.

Frances Hesselbein's Circular Management Revolution

Frances Hesselbein is one of the most respected names in modern leadership, described in 1990 by Peter Drucker as "the best CEO in America," saying that "she could manage any company in America, even General Motors, and do a great job."[15] Keep in mind that when Drucker uttered these words, female CEOs of major organizations were even more rare than today.

Frances was the first CEO of the Girl Scouts of the USA to be chosen from within the organization, rising from volunteer troop leader to council board member and promoted to CEO in 1976, serving until 1990 when she became the founding president of the Peter F. Drucker Foundation for Nonprofit Management. Frances was a longtime client, then friend, mentor, and inspiration to Marshall, who witnessed first-hand the magic of her leadership.

When Frances became CEO, the Girl Scouts organization was in deep trouble. Membership had been on a long, downward spiral before she arrived. In the aftermath of the Vietnam War and the resulting social upheaval of the 1960s, the Girl Scouts were seen as old fashioned and out of touch. Explained Frances, "In the 1960s, we were called square by those who questioned our values."[16]

The solution? Keep the values and bring the Girl Scouts up to date—making the organization cool again and attracting a broader cross section of American girls to join. As part of that effort, Frances enlisted fashion designer Roy Halston as a volunteer to create stylish new uniforms for the scouts and their leaders. She expanded the number of merit badges girls could earn beyond the traditional ones for homemaking and storytelling to achievements in math, science, and technology. She also revamped the existing Girl Scout handbook, persuading a team of artists and educators to modernize it.

When Frances retired from the Girl Scouts in 1990, the organization's downward spiral had been comprehensively reversed. That year, continuing its upward trajectory, total membership was above three million, at the highest level in sixteen years. Nearly 2.5 million girls were participating, with every program level growing for the first time in over two decades. Adult membership reached a historic high.[17]

While Frances's modernization campaign was instrumental to this turnaround, perhaps even more important—and what attracted the attention of Peter Drucker—were the changes she made to the management structure of this staid, hierarchical organization. She implemented a new structure, which she called *circular management*. Frances explains,

> From my own experience from 1976, when I left the mountains of western Pennsylvania to begin my work as CEO of Girl Scouts . . . I knew that the old structures were not right for the next decade, let alone the next century. So volunteers and staff together unleashed our people through a flat, circular, fluid management system.[18]

She wanted to encourage more involvement from all around the organization in leadership. "I truly believe in participatory leadership," she said, "in sharing leadership to the outermost edges of the circle."[19] She wanted all members to feel free to share ideas with and ask questions of the leadership.

Circular Management[20]

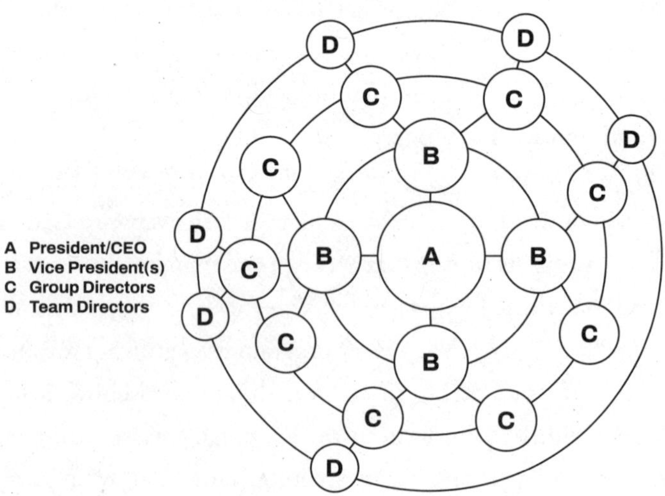

In a *New York Times* article, leadership coach and author Sally Helgesen (with whom Marshall wrote the book *How Women Rise*) tells the story of how Frances described circular management to her one day over lunch, using glasses, cups, a pepper mill, and utensils to link them all. As she revealed the model, Frances told Sally, "The great thing about the circle is it does not box you in. You can connect with any other point. As the circles extend outward, the fabric becomes more interwoven."[21] In other words, the circular management structure opened a wide range of perspectives to Frances and to members across the organization. As Frances explained in a piece she wrote for *Leader to Leader*, "The result was high performance and high morale."[22]

One member who was inspired by Frances's devotion to encouraging input is Mary Ann Altergott. Now a member of the board of directors of the Girl Scouts of the USA and an executive at Edward Jones, she tells the story of how Frances changed the course of her life in the 1980s, when, as a Girl Scout, she was elected to serve on a local council board of directors. Frances was in town to do a council self-assessment, and Mary Ann was invited to join in the conversations. They covered a variety of organizational topics, including performance results, the clarity of operating plans, what the board needed to do to step up, and much more.

Throughout the meetings, Frances encouraged Mary Ann to offer her honest perspective. She recalls Frances telling her, "Your voice matters in this room," and shares, "I felt respected and included, and that's the essence of Girl Scouting . . . What I didn't come to understand until a bit later was that she seeded in me a passion for leadership development, for strategic planning, and for thinking about what was possible versus just what was."[23]

By inviting Mary Ann to the table, encouraging her to speak up, and truly listening to what she had to say, Frances taught everyone there how to be a panoramic leader.

Another of Frances's many contributions was teaching leadership principles to cadets at the United States Military Academy at West Point, which she did every other month for two years. She expanded their maps, bringing other great leaders with her to have a dialogue with the cadets. These executives and leadership thinkers were a great inspiration, and they explained their learnings in ways that enabled the cadets to place them on their maps—effectively microtranslating them.

Frances invited Alan Mulally to join her for one of her West Point classes, and she described how he microtranslated from his own experience to that of the cadets. "Now that's what they're learning in a different language, and you can imagine how it connected with them. He talked a lot about values, a lot about teamwork, a lot about communications. It was totally relevant and it was so skillfully done you weren't aware of the skill, you were aware of the openness, how welcoming he was."[24] He showed through his own example how the cadets gathered before him that day could take what they learned and become panoramic leaders themselves.

From Individual Insight to Organizational Strength: How Piyush Gupta Grew Panoramic Leadership at Scale

When leaders benefit from panoramic leadership, the impact is real. An even greater value emerges when organizations are deliberately built to adopt and sustain the process: consistently taking in perspectives from inside and outside the organization, making sense of change, and acting on it wisely. Few leaders we've met have done this as intentionally as Piyush Gupta, former CEO of DBS Bank, who we introduced in chapter 3, describing how he leveraged optimistic fear into industry-leading AI integration. An even bigger story is how he transformed panoramic leadership from a personal strength into an organizational muscle.

When Piyush took the helm at DBS in 2009, the bank was inward-looking, guided by historical precedent and decades of policy-driven, risk-averse decision-making. Piyush didn't believe that approach would help the company survive the rapid technological disruption, shifting customer expectations, and growing uncertainty that were defining the industry. For DBS to thrive, leaders across the organization would need a wider field of vision that integrated insights from customers, start-ups, other industries, and the broader world.

As Piyush often puts it, one of the core responsibilities of a CEO is "to bring the outside in."[25] But he was also clear that this responsibility couldn't rest only on one person's shoulders. If panoramic leadership depended on the CEO alone, it wouldn't scale. It had to be shared. It had to become an organization-wide capability, embedded in how people and teams thought, learned, and made decisions. What mattered most was creating a reliable cycle: gathering perspectives from the outside, integrating insight internally, and engaging the world with clarity and intent. This wasn't just panoramic leadership in action, but panoramic leadership institutionalized.

To scale the approach, Piyush and his teams architected a multi-level system that created both structural support and cultural permission to look beyond the familiar. Each level reinforced the next, enabling the kind of continuous outside-inside-outside flow that the cycle of panoramic leadership requires—the ongoing refraction of external insight into shared understanding and action.

Level One: Crowd-Sourced Curiosity

At the foundation, DBS created simple but powerful systems, using digital platforms for employees across the organization to surface ideas or share observations about customer behavior, market trends, and practices from other industries. This wasn't a symbolic suggestion box. Resources were allocated to test promising ideas, and when ideas led to visible action, people knew their perspectives mattered. As Piyush emphasized, if ideas "go into a black hole and nothing happens, people stop looking."[26]

Level Two: Accountability and Performance

Next, panoramic leadership was embedded in the company's accountability architecture. DBS organized much of its work through cross-functional teams focused on customer journeys, each led by a journey owner with clear performance metrics. One expectation was explicit: every journey leader had to introduce something meaningfully new each year—an idea microtranslated from another industry, borrowed from a competitor, or inspired by emerging trends. Outside-in thinking wasn't extracurricular. It was part of the job and built directly into leaders' key performance indicators (KPIs). As Piyush explained, this forced leaders "to go and look for things,"[27] not just optimize what they already knew.

Level Three: Horizon Thinking as a Leadership Discipline

The bank was structured into "platforms" based on products and business segments, similar to a classic tech company structure. Each platform was co-led by both a tech leader and a business leader—a structure they called "Two in a Box." Beyond core operations, platform leaders had a clear mandate to look three to five years ahead and explore questions about emerging technologies, evolving products, and global dynamics that could reshape their platform. Importantly, the ideas from this exploration were backed by investments, so long-term thinking wasn't optional. As Piyush noted, the goal wasn't to be right about the future, but to "start asking the what-if questions"[28] that help leaders recognize and respond to it.

Level Four: Scanning the World at the Top of the House

Finally, at the senior-most level, DBS convened regular forums supported by a small research team tasked with scanning the global landscape for technologies, practices from other sectors, and emerging patterns shaping the environment. Twice a year, these forums brought senior leaders together in a focused, collective setting to examine what was changing in the world and decide which ideas deserved attention.

Some moved forward and others were consciously set aside to be revisited in a few years. What mattered most was building a shared habit of mapmaking and exploration into new territory. As Piyush reflected, "The important thing is not what we backed. It's that we built the organizational muscle to keep looking."[29]

Taken together, these four levels transformed DBS into a learning organization that continuously updated its map of the world rather than relying on static assumptions. External insights and perspectives were drawn into the organization's panoramic prism, refracted internally through multiple levels of conversation and experimentation, and then sent back out as new offerings, ways of working, and partnerships.

What made this system work wasn't architecture alone. It was also culture. Piyush was clear that panoramic leadership couldn't be a "we versus they" transformation or a rejection of the organization's past.

Instead, he helped people see something familiar: they were already experimenting and adapting in their personal lives by learning new technologies, navigating unfamiliar systems, and adjusting constantly. The challenge wasn't capability. It was permission.

Through hackathons, cross-generational teams, and hands-on experimentation, employees gained confidence in their ability to learn and contribute. Leaders and teams were recognized for the impact of their panoramic intelligence-driven initiatives. As Piyush observed, when people begin experimenting and aren't punished for thoughtful risk-taking, "a light turns on."[30] Over time, the culture shifted from cautious compliance to curious exploration.

The result was an organization able to absorb uncertainty without paralysis—and make major progress without reckless speed. Panoramic leadership became not just a leadership trait, but a shared language and discipline. Seeing, mapmaking, and adapting became a way of life. What makes this example so powerful is not just the leader himself, but how deliberately the system was designed. And it really paid off. DBS's share price nearly quadrupled during Piyush's tenure, net profit increased fivefold, and both its customer base and workforce grew significantly. It was named the World's Best Bank by Euromoney, the Best Bank in the World by *Global Finance*, and the Global Bank of the Year by *The Banker*. Piyush's example shows that when leaders invest in systems that reward courageous curiosity, encourage connection, and legitimize long-term thinking, they expand their impact far beyond their own line of sight.

What makes this example so powerful is not just the leader himself, but how deliberately the system was designed.

And once people are equipped to see more, connect more, and think further ahead, leaders can begin to do something even more powerful: let go.

That's where the next story begins.

Francine Katsoudas: When Leaders Let Go, New Leaders Grow at Cisco

Francine Katsoudas, Cisco's chief people, policy, and purpose officer and executive vice president, believes that true listening should stretch you. "I find that if you're truly listening, it should be challenging, because you're open to what you're hearing and you're open to having your perspectives change . . . You have to ensure that at any moment, you can pivot based on what you're learning."[31]

When leaders allow themselves to be changed by what they hear, something powerful happens: they model adaptability. They begin to see the world differently, pivoting in response to new understanding, redrawing maps with greater accuracy, and creating space for others to do the same. That's when panoramic leadership begins to scale.

A willingness to let go of control is not a soft skill at Cisco. It's a leadership discipline. It's also crucial to empowering employees as panoramic leaders—people who don't just operate from their own vantage point, but proactively reach out to stakeholders inside and outside of the organization to bring them together, grow their networks, and expand their maps. As Fran puts it, "To enable a team, you have to be willing to not control it."[32]

Cisco's leadership did just that in 2014, when a few new employees in different parts of the United States discovered they were separately supporting Covenant House, a nonprofit organization helping homeless youth, and wanted to start a fundraising initiative at work.

When Cisco's leadership heard about this initiative, they didn't take it over as a corporate program. Instead, they trusted these recently hired young professionals and gave them space to grow their panoramic leadership.

These employees reached out to new colleagues and to Covenant House to understand their perspectives and bring them together. In doing so, they inspired others to join what would become an annual

Cisco tradition: Sleep Out.

During Sleep Out, participants attend an evening gathering focused on youth homelessness, where Covenant House experts and, at times, alumni share powerful stories of survival and hope. After the last conversation concludes, participating employees grab a cardboard box and a clean sleeping bag and head outside for the night, often in cold weather and sometimes in the rain.

The experience is deeply humbling and profoundly eye-opening, creating great empathy for people experiencing homelessness. When participants lie down on cardboard boxes, they let go of their comfort, control of their environment, and preconceived ideas of what it means to be unhoused. They gain a deeper understanding and a more detailed perspective—a reshaped "map"—of the resilience it demands.

What began with only forty-three employees grew more than tenfold, spreading across and beyond the US to Australia, Canada, China, India, Japan, and Mexico. By 2023, Cisco employees had raised substantial funds for Covenant House, totaling $10 million.[33] And Cisco is now an official partner of Covenant House. This grassroots effort became a living example of distributed panoramic leadership. Employees sought perspectives, built alliances, and mobilized action across geographies. Leadership's role was not to centralize the initiative but to protect the space in which it could grow.

By letting go—leaders of control and employees of comfort—Cisco strengthened more than a charitable partnership. It expanded its capacity for panoramic leadership. Across hierarchy and geography, employees practiced reaching outward, integrating perspectives, and translating insight into collective action.

When leaders have the courage to let go, they don't diminish their influence. They widen the organization's field of vision and its capacity to lead.

How Paul Polman Created Ripples of Panoramic Leadership

Paul Polman served as CEO of global consumer goods giant Unilever from 2009 to 2019. A courageous leader, he promoted a stakeholder capitalism-based approach that sought to panoramically connect with every stakeholder involved and advance rigorous goals for improving the well-being of people around the globe while also producing strong profits and shareholder gains.

To make significant progress on these goals, Paul understood that he'd need to align vastly different stakeholders in service of the company's mission, including Unilever employees at all levels, suppliers, community leaders, governmental and nonprofit organizations, the Unilever board, and, of course, the company's investors. He needed to demonstrate this leadership himself while also promoting it across a vast array of individuals with broad-ranging viewpoints and interests—some that were traditionally seen as at odds.

To clarify the company's goals, he and his team developed the Unilever Sustainable Living Plan (USLP). Built on the belief that there was no conflict between sustainability and profitability, this ten-year corporate strategy committed every one of Unilever's many brands to a social and environmental mission.[34] The plan called for three overarching social and environmental outcomes by 2020:

1. "We will help more than a billion people take action to improve their health and well-being.

2. We will decouple our growth from our environmental impact, achieving absolute reductions across the product lifecycle. Our goal is to halve the environmental footprint of the making and use of our products.

3. We will enhance the livelihoods of hundreds of thousands of people in our supply chain."[35]

Paul's approach set in motion a far-reaching movement. When the United Nations put together a working group to develop its Sustainable Development Goals in 2013, Paul was the only business leader from the private sector invited into the group, offering government policy experts and nonprofit leaders important new understandings of for-profit business challenges and capabilities in helping to advance the goals. One specific input was the inclusion in the UN goals of a campaign to promote handwashing, drawing on the long-standing mission of Unilever's Lifebuoy brand of personal care and hygiene products.

A major initiative Paul implemented to cultivate panoramic leadership in his executives was the Partner to Win program. The aim was to develop more innovative and mutually beneficial relationships with Unilever's suppliers. Instead of leaving supplier relationships to corporate buyers, the company asked each of its top fifty executives to personally connect with at least two of its one hundred key suppliers. This broke leaders out of their usual silos and encouraged them to truly understand suppliers' perspectives on working with Unilever while collaborating on ways to support worker well-being across the supply chain. Paul led the way by taking on two suppliers himself.

This proved to be a powerful method of developing company executives' often limited understanding of suppliers, a key stakeholder. Partner to Win paid off for Unilever as suppliers suggested numerous ways to improve products and make them more sustainable, such as laundry detergent that works at lower water temperatures, thereby conserving energy, and shampoo without water to promote water conservation.[36]

Paul emphasized the importance of partnerships—extending beyond suppliers to include a broad range of stakeholders. Those relationships helped rally strong support for Unilever when it was confronted with an unsolicited takeover bid, which many stakeholders feared would nullify the progress the company had made on the USLP.

In February 2017, Kraft Heinz made one of the largest bids in history: $143 billion to acquire Unilever. Just two days later, on Sunday, February 19, 2017, the company withdrew its bid. Unilever had promptly rejected it, stating that it "fundamentally undervalued" the company.[37]

Strikingly, nongovernmental organizations (NGOs) and union leaders, traditional critics of the industry, voiced their support for Unilever. John Sauven, head of Greenpeace UK, which had once scaled Unilever's headquarters in protest, reached out offering help, while Ron Oswald of the IUF, a federation of unions representing ten million workers in the agricultural and hospitality industries, publicly opposed the bid, fearing Unilever's model would be abandoned. Public pressure increased as investors and notable supporters urged Unilever to reject Kraft Heinz's proposal, with some contacting Warren Buffett, a key investor in Kraft Heinz, directly to show their opposition.[38]

As Paul explained in a piece for the *Financial Times*, people were ready to take to YouGov to sign a petition, Bono was ready to write a song to support the fight, and NGOs, unions, pension fund managers, and others were all ready to unite behind Unilever. "There's a whole group of multiple stakeholders that we serve," Paul writes. "This company doesn't belong to us, nor does this company belong to the shareholders in its pure sense."[39]

While the acquisition by one global company of another rarely attracted this much involvement from the wider business ecosystem, because Unilever had formed deep partnerships with a panoramic range of stakeholders, from academics to NGOs, consumers, communities, philanthropies, and investors, they spoke out vigorously.

During his decade at Unilever, Paul not only championed collaboration with stakeholders but also helped them widen their own range of partnerships, allowing them to make a bigger impact and grow their own ripples. The results spoke for themselves: Under Paul's leadership, Unilever was instrumental in driving a sea change in business thinking toward well-being, sustainability, and collective progress—demonstrating that broad stakeholder partnerships are both possible and mutually beneficial. And the company achieved a 290 percent shareholder return during Paul's tenure.[40] As he shared with us, "Leadership is about putting yourself in the service of others, knowing that by doing so you are better off yourself as well."[41]

Ultimately, that's how panoramic leaders achieve their most enduring influence. They change the conversation. The ultimate measure of a leader is not the personal accolades or awards they receive, nor the profits they bring to the bottom line. As we've seen throughout the pages of this book, true leadership transcends individual accomplishment—it ripples out to people, organizations, and communities everywhere.

The Road Ahead

Your sphere of influence is far wider than you may realize. It has the power to create ripple effects that move across organizations and communities, across generations, and around the globe. Panoramic leadership naturally expands to include the growth and empowerment of those around you, shifting the focus from *me* to *we*.

We challenge you to become a catalyst for change—someone who applies the ideas in this book to inspire and equip others with the tools they need to see the wider panorama around them, to connect new dots, and to lead with purpose. When you actively teach, mentor, and guide others—creating an environment where people feel safe to take risks without fear of retribution—you multiply your influence and effectiveness, and you contribute to an ever-expanding circle of panoramic leaders.

The future is in your hands. The ripples begin with you.

QUESTIONS TO CONSIDER

- What specific areas of my life or work offer the greatest potential for my actions to create positive ripple effects?
- How can I guide individuals to develop a greater understanding of different stakeholders and expand their own panoramic intelligence?
- Beyond traditional partnerships, what new alliances or collaborations can I cultivate with a wide array of stakeholders to advance shared goals?
- What potential resistance might I anticipate when trying to broaden perspectives within my own sphere of influence? How will I prepare to address this resistance?
- How can I empower others to further develop their own leadership capabilities?
- How do I envision my current actions creating positive ripples that extend beyond my immediate sphere of influence and help to shape the future?

Acknowledgments

Books begin long before the first word is written. This one began during the quiet moments of my childhood, listening to people whose worlds were nothing like my own, and realizing that perspective isn't a given. It grows through moments that open our eyes—moments the people acknowledged here have so graciously shared with me.

I'm immensely grateful to the leaders whose lives have shaped this work. Thank you for trusting me with your hopes and your successes. My gratitude also extends to the global communities and organizations I've been privileged to work with. Each of you has added an essential perspective to my learning and to this book.

My deep appreciation goes to the leaders I interviewed. Thank you for sharing your journeys with such honesty, for your wisdom, and for your willingness to see the world differently. I feel fortunate to know so many of you, some before writing this book and some whom I was lucky enough to meet through this process.

Marshall Goldsmith, I could not have asked for a more wonderful friend and coauthor. Thank you for your vision to write this book together, for sharing your extraordinary wisdom and guidance, and for believing so deeply in the ideas within it. Your partnership shaped every page.

I've been fortunate to learn from many mentors and supporters who have challenged my perspective and helped me grow, especially Adam Grant, Alan Mulally, Amy Edmondson, Bob Waldinger, Chester Elton, Chris Yeh, Connie Dieken, Dan Pink, Des Dearlove, Dorie Clark, Ferran Adrià, Francine Katsoudas, Guy Kawasaki, Hubert Joly, Keith Ferrazzi, Kenneth Frazier, Lluís Garcia, Paul Polman, Piyush Gupta, Reid Hoffman, Ron Heifetz, Sally Helgesen, Sarah McArthur, Stuart Crainer, Tasha Eurich, and Todd Cherches, as well as Clay Christensen and David Gergen, whose memories remain guiding lights. The number of people who have shaped my thinking is far too great to name fully here. I wish I had a whole book to list everyone who has encouraged and enlightened me. To those mentioned above—and to the many others not named—thank you for your conversations, your lessons, and your gracious support. Each of you has profoundly expanded my understanding of leadership, purpose, and possibility.

Naren Aryal and Amplify Publishing, thank you for your insights in bringing this book into the world. The ideas, encouragement, and steady guidance of your gifted team made the entire process a joy.

Caroline Lambert, Emily Loose, James McCabe, Lari Bishop, and Peter Economy, you transformed this book in pivotal ways and helped me sharpen and articulate ideas that were still finding the right words. What an honor it's been to work on this book together.

My deep gratitude goes to the many partners and collaborators who have walked alongside me and shared so much with me, only some of whom I name here: Harvard University, Helen Krug von Nidda, Oxford HR, Yaron Herman, Yury Boshyk, and all of the extraordinary members of the Marshall Goldsmith 100. Each of you has become an important part of my life and I look forward to continuing to grow together.

Thank you to my brilliant team. Your integrity and curiosity inspire me. You continually broaden my understanding of connection, collaboration, and what leadership can become.

Elizabeth and Robert, my parents, your love has shaped every chapter of my life. Thank you for the grace, courage, and joy with which we've journeyed through life together.

Andrew, Alicia, and Xavier, you are my home no matter where we are in the world. Thank you for holding me steady, for widening my lens when it narrows, and for reminding me that love is life's most expansive perspective. You are, in every sense, my why.

And to you, reader: Thank you for choosing to embark on this journey. May this book widen your view, deepen your understanding, and illuminate pathways you hadn't yet imagined.

Notes

Chapter 1

1 Jacquelyn Smith, "4 Common Reasons Half of All New Executives Fail," World Economic Forum, March 3, 2015, https://www.weforum.org/stories/2015/03/4-common-reasons-half-of-all-new-executives-fail/.

2 Aaron De Smet, Gerald Lackey, and Leigh M. Weiss, "Untangling Your Organization's Decision Making," McKinsey & Company, June 21, 2017, https://www.mckinsey.com/capabilities/people-and-organizational-performance/our-insights/untangling-your-organizations-decision-making.

3 Korn Ferry, "CEO & Board Survey 2025: Risky Business," Korn Ferry Insights, September 5, 2025, https://www.kornferry.com/insights/featured-topics/leadership/ceo-and-board-survey.

4 Cynthia Angell and Krishna Patel, "Origins of the Crisis," *Crisis and Response: An FDIC History, 2008–2013* (Washington, DC: Federal Deposit Insurance Corporation, 2017), https://www.fdic.gov/media/18636.

5 Ben Bernanke, "Reflections on a Year of Crisis: Remarks at the Federal Reserve Bank of Kansas City's Annual Economic Symposium, Jackson Hole, Wyoming," FRASER, August 21, 2009, https://fraser.stlouisfed.org/title/statements-speeches-ben-s-bernanke-453/reflections-a-year-crisis-9045.

6 Ted O'Callahan, "Is the Era of Shareholder Primacy Over?" *Yale Insights*, September 11, 2024, https://insights.som.yale.edu/insights/is-the-era-of-shareholder-primacy-over.

7 Paul Polman and Andrew Winston, "Stakeholder Capitalism Still Makes Business Sense," *Harvard Business Review*, August 21, 2024, https://hbr.org/2024/08/stakeholder-capitalism-still-makes-business-sense.

8 Sarah Vizard, "Lego Ends Marketing Deal with Shell After Greenpeace Campaign," *Marketing Week*, October 14, 2014, https://www.marketingweek.com/lego-ends-marketing-deal-with-shell-after-greenpeace-campaign/.

9 Chris Stokel-Walker, "How Skype Lost Its Crown to Zoom," *Wired*, May 12, 2020, https://www.wired.com/story/skype-coronavirus-pandemic/.

10 Ronald Heifetz, Alexander Grashow, and Marty Linsky, *The Practice of Adaptive Leadership: Tools and Tactics for Changing Your Organization and the World* (Harvard Business Review Press, 2009), 32.

11 Tate, "Cubism," Tate Gallery, n.d., https://www.tate.org.uk/art/art-terms/c/cubism.

Chapter 3

1 Sy Boles, "How Maps (and Cyclists) Paved Way for Roads," *The Harvard Gazette*, January 21, 2025, https://news.harvard.edu/gazette/story/2025/01/how-maps-and-cyclists-paved-the-way-for-roads-harvard-archives-paris/.

2 Ibid.

3 Markham Heid, "Does Thinking Burn Calories? Here's What the Science Says," *Time*, September 19, 2018, https://time.com/5400025/does-thinking-burn-calories/.

4 Marcus Raichle and Debra Gusnard, "Appraising the Brain's Energy Budget," *Proceedings of the National Academy of Sciences USA* (July 29, 2002), https://pmc.ncbi.nlm.nih.gov/articles/PMC124895/.

5 Dorie Clark, *The Long Game: How to Be a Long-Term Thinker in a Short-Term World* (New York: HarperBusiness, 2021), 112.

6 Russell Reynolds Associates, Global CEO Turnover Index. n.d. https://www.russellreynolds.com/en/insights/reports-surveys/global-ceo-turnover-index.

7 Janine Willis and Alexander Todorov, "First Impressions: Making Up Your Mind After a 100-ms Exposure to a Face," *Psychological Science* (July 2006), https://pubmed.ncbi.nlm.nih.gov/16866745/.

8 Alexander Todorov, *Face Value: The Irresistible Influence of First Impressions* (Princeton, NJ: Princeton University Press, 2017), 158.

9 Joseph P. Redden, *Hyperbolic Discounting* (Behavior Lab, Carlson School of Management, University of Minnesota), n.d., http://behaviorlab.org/Papers/Hyperbolic.pdf.

10 Paul Rozin and Edward Royzman, "Negativity Bias, Negativity Dominance, and Contagion," *Personality and Social Psychology Review* (November 2001), https://journals.sagepub.com/doi/10.1207/s15327957pspr0504_2.

11 Chip Heath and Dan Heath, *Decisive* (Currency, 2013), 13.

12 Blockbuster Inc., "Schedule DFAN14A," U.S. Securities and Exchange Commission, April 7, 2005, https://www.sec.gov/Archives/edgar/data/1085734/000092847505000083/0000928475-05-000083.txt.

13 John Antioco, "How I Did It: Blockbuster's Former CEO on Sparring with an Activist Shareholder," *Harvard Business Review*, April 2011, https://hbr.org/2011/04/how-i-did-it-blockbusters-former-ceo-on-sparring-with-an-activist-shareholder.

14 Blockbuster Inc., "Schedule DFAN14A," U.S. Securities and Exchange Commission, April 7, 2005, https://www.sec.gov/Archives/edgar/data/1085734/000092847505000083/0000928475-05-000083.txt.

15 John Antioco, "How I Did It: Blockbuster's Former CEO on Sparring with an Activist Shareholder," Harvard Business Review, April 2011, https://hbr.org/2011/04/how-i-did-it-blockbusters-former-ceo-on-sparring-with-an-activist-shareholder.

16 Mark Gurman and Drake Bennett, "Apple Car's Crash, Design Details, Tim Cook's Indecision, Failed Tesla Deal," *Bloomberg*, March 6, 2024, https://www.bloomberg.com/news/features/2024-03-06/apple-car-s-crash-design-details-tim-cook-s-indecision-failed-tesla-deal.

17 Ibid.

18 HSBC, "Seizing Uncertainty," *HSBC*, n.d., https://www.hsbc.com/seizinguncertainty.

19 BT, "9 in 10 Business Leaders Say Pace of Tech Evolution Is Giving Them 'Byte mares' as BT Warns Tech Anxiety Could Stunt Growth by £11.8 Billion," BT Newsroom, May 13, 2024, https://newsroom.bt.com/9-in-10-business-leaders-say-pace-of-tech-evolution-is-giving-them-bytemares-as-bt-warns-tech-anxiety-could-stunt-growth-by-118b/.

20 Hannah Waters, "The Enchanting Sea Monsters on Medieval Maps," *Smithsonian*, October 15, 2013, https://www.smithsonianmag.com/science-nature/the-enchanting-sea-monsters-on-medieval-maps-1805646.

21 Tim Harper, "Singapore, 1915, and the Birth of the Asian Underground," *Modern Asian Studies*, August 22, 2013, https://www.cambridge.org/core/journals/modern-asian-studies/article/singapore-1915-and-the-birth-of-the-asian-underground/E3097E932B4F60587D9851A77D87AA4C.

22 Thich Nhat Hanh, *Fragrant Palm Leaves: Journals, 1962–1966* (New York: Random House, 2012), 156.

23 Arthur C. Brooks, "Our Brains Are Wired to Pay More Attention to Negative Emotions Than Positive Ones," LinkedIn, n.d., https://www.linkedin.com/posts/arthur-c-brooks_our-brains-are-wired-to-pay-more-attention-activity-7245447202163064832-MkOj.

24 Peter Drucker, *The Effective Executive* (Harper Collins e-books, 2009), 51.

25 Ben Sherry, "Some Employees Are 'Sabotaging' Their Company's AI Strategy, According to a New Survey," *Inc.*, March 19, 2025, https://www.inc.com/ben-sherry/employees-are-sabotaging-their-companys-ai-strategy-according-to-a-new-survey/91162740.

26 Thomas Davenport and Randy Bean, "Portrait of an AI Leader: Piyush Gupta of DBS Bank," *MIT Sloan Management Review*, August 31, 2021, https://sloanreview.mit.edu/article/portrait-of-an-ai-leader-piyush-gupta-of-dbs-bank/.

Chapter 4

1 Ray Kroc, *Grinding It Out* (1977; reprinted New York: St. Martin's Press, 2016), 123.

2 Jay Rayner, "If the World's Greatest Chef Cooked for a Living, He'd Starve," *The Guardian*, December 10, 2006, https://www.theguardian.com/observer/foodmonthly/futureoffood/story/0,,1969713,00.html.

3 Ferran Adrià, "Arrival at el Bulli, 'Act One,'" The Years of Learning, el Bulli Foundation—History, *La historia de El Bulli: 1961–2006* (ElBulli.com), n.d., http://elbulli.com/historia/version_imprimible/1961-2006_en.pdf.

4 *La historia de El Bulli: 1961–2006*, "Historia" section, ElBulli.com, n.d., http://elbulli.com/historia/index.php?lang=en&seccion=3&subseccion=2.

5 Ferran Adrià, interview by Cornelia Choe, October 30, 2024, conducted in Spanish.

6 Colman Andrews, *Ferran: The Inside Story of El Bulli and the Man Who Reinvented Food* (Gotham, 2010), 26.

7 Ferran Adrià, interview by Cornelia Choe, October 30, 2024, conducted in Spanish.

8 Ibid.

9 Ibid.

10 Ibid.

11 Tristan Gooley, "The Why and How of Natural Navigation," TEDxCalgary, November 2018, https://www.ted.com/talks/tristan_gooley_the_why_and_how_of_natural_navigation.

12 Carol S. Dweck, "The Perils and Promises of Praise," *Educational Leadership* 65, no. 2 (October 2007): 34.

13 Ibid.

14 Adam Grant, *Think Again* (Viking, 2021), 59.

15 Patty McCord, *Powerful: Building a Culture of Freedom and Responsibility* (Silicon Guild, 2018), 57.

16 Frank DePhillips, William Berliner, and James Cribbin, *Management of Training Programs* (Richard D. Erwin, Inc., 1960), 69.

17 Ibid.

18 Tasha Eurich, *Insight* (Portfolio, 2017), 65.

19 Greg Bishop, "Serena Williams Loses in First Round," *New York Times*, May 29, 2012, http://www.nytimes.com/2012/05/30/sports/tennis/2012-french-open-serena-williams-ousted-in-first-round.html.

20 Mirren Gidda, "Can a Controversial Coach Help Serena Williams Stay the World's Best Tennis Player?" *Newsweek*, June 19, 2016, http://www.newsweek.com/patrick-mouratoglou-serena-williams-coach-471758.

21 Barry O'Reilly, *Unlearn: Let Go of Past Success to Achieve Extraordinary Results* (McGraw Hill, 2018), 8.

22 Steve Flink, "That Championship Season: Serena Williams Caps a Sizzling Summer, 2012," US Open, August 22, 2022, https://www.usopen.org/en_US/news/articles/2022-08-22/that_championship_season_serena_williams_caps_a_sizzling_summer_2012.html.

Chapter 5

1 Michael Distefano, "Alan Mulally: The Man Who Saved Ford," Korn Ferry, August 10, 2014, https://www.kornferry.com/insights/briefings-magazine/issue-20/alan-mulally-man-who-saved-ford.

2 Lean Leaper, "People-First Leadership: A Conversation Between Jim Morgan and Alan Mulally," Lean Enterprise Institute, September 1, 2021, https://www.lean.org/the-lean-post/articles/people-first-leadership-a-conversation-between-jim-morgan-and-alan-mulally/.

3 Steve Finlay, "And He Threw in Floor Mats," WardsAuto, May 1, 2007, https://www.wardsauto.com/ford/and-he-threw-in-floor-mats.

4 "Working Together Webinar with Alan Mulally and Marshall Goldsmith," YouTube video, posted by *Marshall Goldsmith*, March 8, 2021, https://www.youtube.com/watch?v=vYWMBhbLggA.

5 Lean Leaper, "People-First Leadership: A Conversation Between Jim Morgan and Alan Mulally," Lean Enterprise Institute, September 1, 2021, https://www.lean.org/the-lean-post/articles/people-first-leadership-a-conversation-between-jim-morgan-and-alan-mulally/.

6 Dave Wilson, "How Alan Mulally Taught Me to S.E.R.V.E.," PR Web, n.d., https://www.prweb.com/releases/how_alan_mulally_taught_me_to_s_e_r_v_e_/prweb14784719.htm.

7 Jacinda Ardern, "Prime Minister Jacinda Ardern Announces Resignation," Government of New Zealand, January 19, 2023, Beehive.govt.nz, https://www.beehive.govt.nz/release/prime-minister-jacinda-ardern-announces-resignation.

8 Indra Nooyi, *My Life in Full: Work, Family, and Our Future* (Portfolio, 2021), 222.

9 Ibid., 230–232.

10 Brené Brown, *Daring Greatly: How the Courage to Be Vulnerable Transforms the Way We Live, Love, Parent, and Lead* (New York: Gotham Books, 2012), 253.

11 Nicholas Epley and Juliana Schroeder, "Mistakenly Seeking Solitude," *Journal of Experimental Psychology: General* (2014), https://psycnet.apa.org/doiLanding?doi=10.1037%2Fa0037323.

12 "Mom Was Wrong: You Should Talk to Strangers," press release, The University of Chicago Booth School of Business, July 17, 2014, https://www.chicagobooth.edu/media-relations-and-communications/press-releases/mom-was-wrong-you-should-talk-to-strangers.

13 "How Design Thinking Transformed Airbnb from a Failing Startup to a Billion Dollar Business," *First Round Review*, accessed October 10, 2025, https://review.firstround.com/how-design-thinking-transformed-airbnb-from-failing-startup-to-billion-dollar-business/.

14 Arthur C. Brooks, "Compatibility Keeps Us Connected — But It's ...," LinkedIn, n.d., https://www.linkedin.com/posts/arthur-c-brooks_compatibility-keeps-us-connected-but-its-activity-7246176129609277440-5tQq.

15 Heidi Godman, "Do Parasocial Relationships Fill a Loneliness Gap?" Harvard Health Publishing, September 30, 2024, https://www.health.harvard.edu/blog/do-parasocial-relationships-fill-a-loneliness-gap-202409303074.

16 Maria Popova and Claudia Bedrick, eds., *A Velocity of Being: Letters to a Young Reader* (Enchanted Lion Books, 2018), 28.

17 R. Surujnarain, *Leakey and Goodall: Scientists Who Changed How We Define 'Human,'* Jane Goodall's Good for All News, August 7, 2019, https://news.janegoodall.org/2019/08/07/7138/.

18 National Geographic Society, "Jane Goodall," *National Geographic Education*, n.d., https://education.nationalgeographic.org/resource/jane-goodall/.

19 Jane Goodall Institute, *Jane Goodall: The Woman Who Redefined Man and Chimpanzees*, n.d., https://www.janegoodall.org/wp-content/uploads/the-Jane-Goodall-Institute_JaneGoodall_LongBio.pdf.

20 Jack Sim, interview by Cornelia Choe, June 30, 2024.

21 World Toilet Organization, "About Us," World Toilet Organization, n.d., https://worldtoilet.org/web-agency-gb-about-us/.

22 World Health Organization and United Nations Children's Fund, *Progress on Household Drinking-Water, Sanitation and Hygiene 2000–2024: Special Focus on Inequalities* (Geneva: World Health Organization, August 26, 2025), https://www.who.int/publications/m/item/progress-on-household-drinking-water--sanitation-and-hygiene-2000-2024--special-focus-on-inequalities.

23 "Sanitation," World Health Organization, March 22, 2024, https://www.who.int/news-room/fact-sheets/detail/sanitation.

24 Jack Sim, interview by Cornelia Choe, June 30, 2024.

25 Ibid.

26 Ben Unglesbee, "'Listen to the Frontline': Hubert Joly on the Art of the Turnaround at Best Buy," Retail Dive, June 25, 2021, https://www.retaildive.com/news/listen-to-the-frontline-hubert-joly-on-the-art-of-the-turnaround-at-best/602455/.

27 Hubert Joly with Caroline Lambert, *The Heart of Business: Leadership Principles for the Next Era of Capitalism* (Harvard Business Review Press, 2021), 45.

28 Ibid., 61.

29 Ibid., 47.

30 Ibid., 114.

31 Ibid., 213.

Chapter 6

1 National Museum of Australia, "Four World Maps," n.d., https://www.nma.gov.au/explore/collection/highlights/four-world-maps.

2 John Robson, "Why Did James Cook Join the Royal Navy in 1755?" Captain Cook Society, 2005, https://www.captaincooksociety.com/cooks-voyages/early-voyages/early-royal-navy-voyages/why-did-james-cook-join-the-royal-navy-in-1755.

3 Lily Katzman, "250 Years Ago, Joseph Banks Documented Australia's Glorious Botanical Bounty," *Smithsonian*, February 26, 2020, https://www.smithsonianmag.com/smithsonian-institution/250-years-ago-joseph-banks-documented-australias-glorious-botanical-bounty-180974245/.

4 Ian Boreham, "July-September 1769," Captain Cook Society, 2019, https://www.captaincooksociety.com/cooks-voyages/first-pacific-voyage/july-september-1769.

5 Laura Heller, "See Dick Get No Respect: Why Best Buy's Founder Is Fighting for His Company," *Forbes*, August 6, 2012, https://www.forbes.com/sites/lauraheller/2012/08/06/see-dick-get-no-respect-why-best-buys-founder-is-fighting-a-battle-for-his-company/.

6 Hubert Joly with Caroline Lambert, *The Heart of Business: Leadership Principles for the Next Era of Capitalism* (Harvard Business Review Press, 2021), 237.

7 Ibid., 117.

8 Ibid., 118.

9 Ibid., 101–102.

10 Ibid., 103.

11 Wynton Marsalis, "Democracy, Culture, and Civil Society," Institute of Politics Harvard Kennedy School, February 10, 2025, https://www.youtube.com/watch?v=uC6msaBihiM.

12 Terry Szuplat, *Say It Well: Find Your Voice, Speak Your Mind, Inspire Any Audience* (Harper Business, 2024), 68–69.

13 Aparna Bharadwaj, "Hidden Connections That Transcend Borders and Defy Stereotypes," TED, January 28, 2023, https://www.youtube.com/watch?v=n1fL-EdTsTI.

14 George Kohlrieser, Susan Goldsworthy, and Duncan Coombe, *Care to Dare: Unleashing Astonishing Potential Through Secure Base Leadership* (Jossey-Bass, 2012), 4–5.

15 Amy Edmondson, *The Fearless Organization* (Wiley, 2019), xiii-xv.

16 Bryce Hoffman, *American Icon: Alan Mulally and the Fight to Save Ford Motor Company* (Crown Business, 2012), 104.

17 Marc A. Feigen, Michael Jenkins, and Anton Warendh, "Is It Time to Consider Co-CEOs?" *Harvard Business Review*, July-August 2022, https://hbr.org/2022/07/is-it-time-to-consider-co-ceos.

18 Amy Wallace, "Inside Netflix's Unusual Co-CEO Arrangement—and Why It Works," *Fast Company*, September 9, 2024, https://www.fastcompany.com/91177003/netflix-ceo-co-ted-sarandos-greg-peters-culture-coach.

19 Alan Mulally, interview by Cornelia Choe, April 4, 2025.

20 Ashley Gross, "Former Boeing Executive Alan Mulally's Advice on Labor: 'Working Together Works,'" KNKX, October 15, 2014, https://www.knkx.org/business/2014-10-15/former-boeing-executive-alan-mulallys-advice-on-labor-working-together-works.

Chapter 7

1 "Trench Warfare," The National WWI Museum and Memorial, n.d., https://www.theworldwar.org/learn/about-wwi/trench-warfare.

2 Swift Geospatial, "The Evolution of GIS: Aerial Photography and the Mapping Revolution (Part 1)," January 23, 2025, https://swiftgeospatial.solutions/2025/01/23/the-evolution-of-gis-aerial-photography-and-the-mapping-revolution-1/.

3 "How to Look for Records of...Military Maps of the First World War," The National Archives, n.d., https://www.nationalarchives.gov.uk/help-with-your-research/research-guides/military-maps-first-world-war/.

4 S. McArthur, A. Mulally, D. Dornseif, M. Lombardi, et al., "People 'Working Together'© to Produce the Preferred Boeing 777 Airplane Family," *Leader to Leader*, May 19, 2025, https://onlinelibrary.wiley.com/doi/10.1002/ltl.20891.

5 "How Superstar CEO Alan Mulally Brought Ford Back from the Brink," Acertitude, n.d., https://www.acertitude.com/insights/how-superstar-ceo-alan-mulally-brought-ford-back-from-the-brink.

6 James Cook, "Journals, Volume 1, The Voyage of the Endeavour, 1768–1771" (Cambridge University Press, 1969), 154.

7 Cristy Gelling, "Reading a Pacific Navigator's Mysterious Map May Require a Shift in Perspective," *Knowable*, December 23, 2021, https://knowablemagazine.org/content/article/society/2021/reading-pacific-navigators-mysterious-map.

8 Ibid.

9 Lars Eckstein and Anja Schwarz, "The Making of Tupaia's Map: A Story of the Extent and Mastery of Polynesian Navigation, Competing Systems of Wayfinding on James Cook's *Endeavour*, and the Invention of an Ingenious Cartographic System," *The Journal of Pacific History* 54, no. 1 (2018): 1–95, https://doi.org/10.1080/00223344.2018.1512369.

10 Laura Böhm, "Tupaia's Map," University of Potsdam, March 29, 2023, https://www.uni-potsdam.de/en/iaa-alc/tupaias-map#c455946.

11 Lars Eckstein and Anja Schwarz, "The Making of Tupaia's Map: A Story of the Extent and Mastery of Polynesian Navigation, Competing Systems of Wayfinding on James Cook's *Endeavour*, and the Invention of an Ingenious Cartographic System," *The Journal of Pacific History* 54, no. 1 (2018): 1–95, https://doi.org/10.1080/00223344.2018.1512369.

12 Punua Tamaehu, interview by Cornelia Choe, July 26, 2024, conducted in French.

13 Ronald Heifetz, Alexander Grashow, and Marty Linsky, *The Practice of Adaptive Leadership: Tools and Tactics for Changing Your Organization and the World* (Harvard Business Review Press, 2009), 122–123.

14 Ibid., 245.

15 Ibid., 242.

16 Hubert Joly with Caroline Lambert, *The Heart of Business: Leadership Principles for the Next Era of Capitalism* (Harvard Business Review Press, 2021), 126–128.

17 Ibid., 183-184.

18 Ibid., 63.

19 "Steering Through the Business Storm: Leadership Lessons from Best Buy's Former CEO, Hubert Joly," HEC Paris, October 23, 2023, https://www.hec.edu/en/executive-education/news/steering-through-business-storm-leadership-lessons-best-buy-s-former-ceo-hubert-joly.

Chapter 8

1 Bernardo Javalquinto Lagos, "The Leadership Role in Mergers and Acquisitions: A Thorough Examination of Crucial Elements for Business Success," SSRN, posted July 12, 2025, https://papers.ssrn.com/sol3/papers.cfm?abstract_id=5337874.

2 Alan Mulally, interview by Cornelia Choe, April 4, 2025.

Chapter 9

1 Parth Patil, interview by Cornelia Choe, January 2, 2025.

2 Alan Mulally, interview by Cornelia Choe, April 4, 2025.

3 "How the Story Transforms the Teller," YouTube video, 14:38, posted by TEDx Talks, May 15, 2018, https://www.youtube.com/watch?v=wgeh4xhSA2Q.

4 Ibid.

5 Robert Waldinger, "Robert Waldinger: What Makes a Good Life? Lessons from the Longest Study on Happiness," TED, January 25, 2016, https://www.youtube.com/watch?v=8KkKuTCFvzI.

6 "Our Epidemic of Loneliness and Isolation," US Department of Health and Human Services, 2023, https://www.hhs.gov/sites/default/files/surgeon-general-social-connection-advisory.pdf.

7 Robert Waldinger and Marc Schulz, *The Good Life: Lessons from the World's Longest Scientific Study of Happiness* (Simon & Schuster, 2023), 101.

8 George W. Bush Presidential Center, "Arthur Brooks — The Science of Happiness," *Bush Center*, n.d., https://www.bushcenter.org/publications/arthur-brooks-the-science-of-happiness.

9 Yasmeen A. Khan and Jeffrey Q. Yang, "Arthur Brooks on How to Be Happy," *The Harvard Crimson*, November 3, 2022, https://www.thecrimson.com/article/2022/11/3/arthur-brooks-happiness/.

10 Ibid.

11 "Giving Thanks Can Make You Happier," Harvard Health Publishing, August 14, 2021, https://www.health.harvard.edu/healthbeat/giving-thanks-can-make-you-happier.

12 Chester Elton and Adrian Gostick, *Leading with Gratitude: Eight Leadership Practices for Extraordinary Business Results* (Harper Business, 2020), 189.

13 Emma Seppälä, "How to Apply the Science of Happiness to Accelerate Your Success," The Center for Compassion and Altruism Research and Education, January 15, 2016, https://ccare.stanford.edu/uncategorized/how-to-apply-the-science-of-happiness-to-accelerate-your-success/.

14 Guy Kawasaki, *Wiser Guy: Lessons from a Life* (New York: Portfolio/Penguin, 2019), 197.

15 Robert Waldinger and Marc Schulz, *The Good Life: Lessons from the World's Longest Scientific Study of Happiness* (Simon & Schuster, 2023), 49–50.

Chapter 10

1 Thich Nhat Hanh, *Understanding Our Mind: 50 Verses on Buddhist Psychology* (Parallax Press, 2002), 227.

2 Indra Nooyi, "Meet Indra," IndraNooyi.com, n.d., https://www.indranooyi.com/meetindra.

3 Indra Nooyi, *My Life in Full: Work, Family, and Our Future* (Portfolio, 2021), 198.

4 Daniel H. Pink, *Drive: The Surprising Truth About What Motivates Us* (New York: Riverhead Books, 2009), 131.

5 Indra Nooyi and Vijay Govindarajan, "Becoming a Better Corporate Citizen," *Harvard Business Review*, March-April 2020, https://hbr.org/2020/03/becoming-a-better-corporate-citizen.

6 Ibid.

7 Indra Nooyi, *My Life in Full: Work, Family, and Our Future* (Portfolio, 2021), 204–5.

8 Ibid., 229–230.

9 Ibid., 211.

10 Indra Nooyi, "It's Time for Leaders to Care (Part 2)." *ReThinking with Adam Grant* (podcast), TED Audio Collective, November 2, 2021, https://www.ted.com/pages/indra-nooyi-time-for-leaders-to-care-part-2-transcript.

11 Ibid.

12 Shu Wen Ng, Meghan M. Slining, and Barry M. Popkin, "The Healthy Weight Commitment Foundation Pledge: Calories Sold from U.S. Consumer Packaged Goods, 2007–2012," *Am J Prev Med* 47, no. 4 (October 2014): 508–519, doi:10.1016/j.amepre.2014.05.029, https://pmc.ncbi.nlm.nih.gov/articles/PMC4171694/.

13 Dave Wilson, "How Alan Mulally Taught Me to S.E.R.V.E.," PR Web, n.d., https://www.prweb.com/releases/how_alan_mulally_taught_me_to_s_e_r_v_e_/prweb14784719.htm.

14 Ibid.

15 Elizabeth Edersheim, "The Woman Peter Drucker Said Was the Best CEO in America," Corporate Learning Network, October 28, 2021, https://www.corporatelearningnetwork.com/leadership/articles/the-woman-peter-drucker-said-was-the-best-ceo-in-america.

16 Scott Smith, "Frances Hesselbein Led Dramatic Girl Scout Turnaround," *Investor's Business Daily*, February 2, 2016, https://www.investors.com/news/management/leaders-and-success/frances-hesselbein-teaches-army-leadership/.

17 *The Girl Scouts of the USA, Annual Report*, 1990, https://archives.girlscouts.org/Detail/objects/5576.

18 S. Jacobson, *Managing in a World That Is Round by Frances Hesselbein, Leader to Leader*, 2022, https://www.leadertoleader.org/managing-in-a-world-that-is-round-by-frances-hesselbein/.

19 Laurel Shaper Walters, "A Leader Redefines Management," *Christian Science Monitor*, September 22, 1992, https://www.csmonitor.com/1992/0922/22141.html.

20 Frances Hesselbein, *My Life in Leadership: The Journey and Lessons Learned Along the Way* (Jossey-Bass, 2011), 86.

21 Sally Helgesen, "The Pyramid and the Web," *The New York Times*, May 27, 1990, https://www.nytimes.com/1990/05/27/business/forum-the-pyramid-and-the-web.html.

22 Frances Hesselbein, "Managing in a World That Is Round," *Leader to Leader*, Fall 1996, https://web.archive.org/web/20061130083940/http://leadertoleader.org/leaderbooks/L2L/fall96/fh.html.

23 "Frances Hesselbein Friendship Room Dedication," YouTube video, June 27, 2022, https://www.youtube.com/watch?v=geWOqXEraXI.

24 Frances Hesselbein and Philip Scarpino, "Frances Hesselbein," Tobias Leadership Center, March 4, 2011, https://tobiascenter.iu.edu/research/oral-history/audio-transcripts/hesselbein-frances.html.

25 Piyush Gupta, interview by Cornelia Choe, January 8, 2026.

26 Ibid.

27 Ibid.

28 Ibid.

29 Ibid.

30 Ibid.

31 Francine Katsoudas, LinkedIn post, March 8, 2023, https://www.linkedin.com/posts/forbes-magazine_francine-katsoudas-spoke-about-creating-culture-activity-7039135482835832832-a_R8/.

32 Francine Katsoudas, interview by Cornelia Choe, November 1, 2024.

33 Cisco Systems, Inc., Purpose Report 2023 (San Jose, CA: Cisco Systems, Inc., 2023), https://www.cisco.com/c/dam/m/en_us/about/purpose/reporting-hub/_pdf/purpose-report-2023.pdf.

34 "Unilever Sustainable Living Plan: Small Actions. Big Difference," Unilever, 2010, https://www.unilever.com/files/origin/9752ff2d82b8afabb507eb92c47b5dad795801d5.pdf/unilever-sustainable-living-plan.pdf.

35 Ibid.

36 Paul Polman and Andrew Wilson, *Net Positive* (Harvard Business Review Press, 2021), 319–321.

37 Unilever N.V., *Minutes of the Annual General Meeting 2017*, remarks by Chairman Marijn Dekkers, p. 2, n.d., https://www.unilever.com/files/92ui5egz/production/d01826f8be9dd7a5c8324e36d4715c530eafc22c.pdf.

38 Paul Polman and Andrew Wilson, *Net Positive* (Harvard Business Review Press, 2021), 23.

39 Paul Polman, "Paul Polman: In His Own Words," *Financial Times*, December 3, 2017, https://www.ft.com/content/2209d63a-d6ae-11e7-8c9a-d9c0a5c8d5c9.

40 CNBC, "Paul Polman," n.d., https://www.cnbc.com/paul-polman.

41 Paul Polman, email message to Cornelia Choe, September 8, 2025; and Paul Polman, interview by Cornelia Choe, September 16, 2025.

LEADERSHIP IN CONVERSATION

Panoramic Leadership in Practice

Alan Mulally's leadership journey reflects the power of perspective, alignment, and execution.

In this conversation, Alan Mulally, Sarah McArthur, Cornelia Choe, and Marshall Goldsmith explore how panoramic leadership shapes decisions, culture, and organizational success.

Scan to watch the full conversation.

About the Authors

Cornelia Choe is an international leadership expert, keynote speaker, and top-tier executive coach. A Thinkers50 Radar honoree, she is recognized as one of the world's most influential management thinkers. She is the founder and CEO of The Leaders Alliance, an organization that empowers CEOs and C-suite leaders across five continents.

Drawing on a career spanning multilateral institutions, government agencies, and global companies, from start-ups to Fortune 500 corporations, Cornelia advises leaders navigating rapid change and organizational transformation. Her work is grounded in a deep understanding of human dynamics and intergroup communication, helping individuals and organizations widen their perspectives, strengthen alignment, and unlock collective potential.

Cornelia's upbringing across three continents and her life in seven countries shaped her commitment to bridging perspectives and fostering meaningful human connection. At eighteen, she led a groundbreaking initiative linking CEOs across continents, reinforcing her belief in the power of collective support. A year later, she was invited to speak at a landmark United Nations conference on development, change management, and leadership—an experience that propelled her onto the world stage. Today, she speaks globally, delivering keynote addresses that help leaders navigate rapid change and shape a more connected future.

She studied political science at Georgetown University and earned a master's degree from the Harvard Kennedy School. Before founding The Leaders Alliance, she invested in and supported leadership teams across Asia, Europe, and North America while working with private equity funds at Morgan Stanley and other institutions. These experiences deepened her expertise in guiding leaders through international growth and change.

Fluent in three languages, Cornelia builds connections across cultures and sectors. Her work focuses on helping leaders shape the future through transformative change and a panoramic view of what is possible.

Dr. Marshall Goldsmith is a member of the *Thinkers50* Hall of Fame and the only two-time *Thinkers50* number one Leadership Thinker in the World. He has been ranked as the world's number one executive coach and a top ten business thinker for years. His clients have included over two hundred global CEOs, and his writing, speaking, and coaching have impacted tens of millions of leaders around the world.

A *New York Times* number one bestselling author, his fifty-five books have sold over three million copies and have been translated into thirty-five languages. In 2023, both *Chief Executive* magazine and *Thinkers50* listed *What Got You Here Won't Get You There* as one of the best business books ever written. Amazon listed it, along with *Triggers*, in 100 Best Leadership & Success Books of All Time. Marshall is the only living author with two books on the list. His newest book, and fourth *NYT* bestseller, is *The Earned Life*.

Marshall's acknowledgments include *Business Week*'s 50 Great Leaders in America, Institute for Management Studies' Lifetime Award for Teaching, *Harvard Business Review*'s World's number one Leadership Thinker, American Management Association's 50 Great Thinkers Who Have Influenced the Field of Management, SHRM Linkage's Legends of Leadership Award, and Global Gurus' Corps d'Elite Award for Lifetime Contribution in Leadership and Coaching. His life is featured in the documentary *The Earned Life* and *The New Yorker* profile "The Better Boss."

Dr. Goldsmith served as a professor of Management Practice at the Dartmouth Tuck School of Business. He holds a PhD from the UCLA Anderson School of Management, where he received the John E. Anderson Distinguished Alumni Award; an MBA from the Indiana University Kelley School of Business, where he received the Distinguished Entrepreneur Award; and a BS from Rose-Hulman Institute of Technology, where he received an honorary PhD in engineering in 2023. He has been a volunteer adviser and coach for leaders at the Peter Drucker Foundation, World Bank, St. Jude Children's Research Hospital, US Army and Navy, Girl Scouts of America, USAID, and International and American Red Cross, where he was a National Volunteer of the Year.

Hundreds of Dr. Goldsmith's articles, interviews, columns, and videos are available free online.